Qigong and Tai Chi

Harnessing Your Chi Energy and Unlocking the Power of an Internal Chinese Martial Art

Your Free Gift (only available for a limited time)

Thanks for getting this book! If you want to learn more about various spirituality topics, then join Mari Silva's community and get a free guided meditation MP3 for awakening your third eye. This guided meditation mp3 is designed to open and strengthen ones third eye so you can experience a higher state of consciousness. Simply visit the link below the image to get started.

https://spiritualityspot.com/meditation

Contents

Part 1: Qigong

An Essential Beginner's Guide to Developing Your Chi and Cultivating Healing Energy

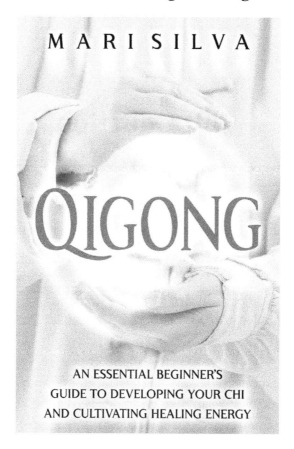

M A R I S I L V A

QIGONG

AN ESSENTIAL BEGINNER'S
GUIDE TO DEVELOPING YOUR CHI
AND CULTIVATING HEALING ENERGY

Introduction

There's a reason why Qigong has been around for centuries and continues to grow in popularity worldwide. Qigong supports optimal health and well-being. The ancient Traditional Chinese medicine practice is an all-natural and cost-efficient way to enjoy abundant energy and vitality. In this book, you will learn all there is to know about this ancient practice so you can start incorporating it into your daily life and enjoy its wonderful effects.

Why should you read this book? It's simple. I've written it with beginners in mind. While it covers practically all bases of the practice, it's a book that explains all the important aspects of Qigong in an easy-to-understand manner. More importantly, you'll be able to start practicing it as soon as you're done reading. To ensure this, the final chapter gives you a practical and simple daily routine. From theoretical to practical, this book has you covered.

If you're ready, turn the page, and let's begin.

Chapter 1: The Art and Benefits of Qigong

The word Qigong comes from two Chinese characters representing the words chi and gong. Chi refers to here, breath, or gas. Often, it's translated into a metaphysical form called vital energy. This energy is intended to circulate throughout the entire body. She can also be generally defined as a universal energy that includes electromagnetic, light, and heat energy. Being the central foundational principle in traditional Chinese medicine and martial arts, various definitions of the word often include breathing, air, and the interactions between spirit, energy, and matter.

Gong, or "Kung," on the other hand, is often interpreted as work. Many people define it as a specific form of practice, accomplishment, result, service, achievement, merit, or mastery. People also use the word to refer to gong fu, also known as Kung Fu, as a way to express effort that leads to accomplishment.

Combining these two words, Qigong describes a particular practice or way of doing things that help promote health and well-being through the cultivation and balancing of life energy.

During the 1940s and 1950s, Qigong was a word used to describe a wide range of Chinese exercises that focused on health and science. People have started to gradually shift their focus away from its original Chinese roots, i.e., the spiritual practices and mysticism.

History of Qigong

Qigong is an ancient Chinese practice that has been around for over 4000 years. Throughout its rich history, many Qigong practices have been developed throughout different societal segments in Chinese culture. These include:

1. Confucianism: moral character development and longevity are the main focus

2. Chinese martial arts: if the objective is to develop excellent fighting abilities

3. Traditional Chinese medicine: the main goal is the cure or prevention of illnesses and ailments

4. Buddhism and Daoism: it uses Qigong as an integrative part of meditation

Today, modern Qigong combines many different traditions. Often, these are diverse or even disparate. A good example of this is combining Daoism's internal alchemy meditative practice with the ancient standing meditation practice of shing chi or circulating chi, the standing meditation practice called Zhan Zhuang, and the Dao Yin breathing exercise called guiding and pulling.

Normally, Qigong masters taught the practice to their students verbally and through actual training. In particular, they emphasized scholarly meditation practices together with dynamic or gymnastic practices used by many people in Chinese society.

But beginning in the late 40s and throughout the 1950s, The Chinese Communist Party government attempted to combine the many different forms of the practice to establish credible scientific bases for Qigong. For example, Liu Guizhen established Qigong as a set of life-enhancing practices better founded on many philosophical traditions such as the Dao Yin. For many experts, this was the start of the modernization of the sanctification of Qigong.

From 1958 to 1963, the period popularly known as the Great Leap Forward, and during The Cultural Revolution from 1966 to 1976, the Communist Party imposed a tight rein over the practice. Along with other Traditional Chinese medical practices, public access to Qigong was severely limited through very tight controls. In government-run rehabilitation centers, the practice was promoted. As a result, Qigong continued to spread throughout China through hospitals and universities. Once the Cultural Revolution ended, Qigong became even more popular as a daily morning exercise practiced by throngs of people throughout the country.

After the death of Mao Zedong, Qigong became even more popular during Deng Xiaoping and Jiang Xiemin's reign from 1976 through much of the 1990s. During this time, anywhere from 60 to 200 million Chinese citizens were performing Qigong throughout the nation. As it became more popular, controversies and problems also started popping up. These include:

1. Qigong deviation, which was considered as a mental condition

2. Using pseudoscience in establishing Qigong practitioner credibility

3. The creation of many cults centered on the practice

4. Exaggerated claims of extraordinary capabilities, many of which may be classified as out of this world

5. So-called Qigong masters exaggerating their claims to benefit from the practice personally

The Chinese government established the national Chi Gong Science and Research Organization in 1985 to properly regulate the numerous Qigong-related denominations that have sprouted all over the country. The Chinese government finally enforced control measures on the public practice of Qigong in 1999 in reaction to the continued spreading of the practice, which resulted in the massive revival of old Chinese traditions that authorities felt were a threat, such as

1. Morality

2. Spirituality

3. Mysticism

Part of the public control measures implemented on Qigong practitioners includes - closing clinics and hospitals that promoted the practice as part of their healing protocols and banning groups that promote the same such as Falun gong. Ever since the implementation of crackdowns, The Chinese government has only supported the research and practice of Qigong as part of traditional Chinese medicine. Any context related to spirituality and other non-health and medical contexts continues to be rejected.

In line with this approach, The Chinese Communist Party or CCP created the Chinese Health Qigong Association in 2000. This regulatory body tightly controls the public practice of Qigong by:

1. Limiting Qigong related public gatherings

2. Requiring instructors to be trained and certified by the government

3. Restricting Qigong practices to those that the government approves

Despite strict government measures, Qigong managed to spread worldwide because of three factors; The Chinese diaspora, globalization, and the rapid growth of the tourism industry in China. As a result, billions of people regularly practice Qigong, believing in its many benefits. Just like how it started, global citizens who have adopted Qigong as part of their lifestyle come in a wide range of nationalities and races. They do so for a myriad number of reasons, which include:

1. Recreation

2. Physical fitness

3. Preventive health

4. Alleviation of sicknesses and many medical conditions

5. Martial arts training

6. Spiritual growth

7. Meditation

General Qigong Practices

Based on ancient Chinese philosophy, Qigong covers a wide range of practices that aim to develop excellent coordination between a person's body, mind, and breath. These include meditation (both still and moving), chanting, massage, non-contact treatments, and sound meditation. All of these are performed using a wide variety of body postures.

Typically, Qigong can be classified into two main categories: active or dynamic Qigong and passive or meditative Qigong. Active Qigong, also known as Dong gong, is performed with slow but flowing movements. But passive Qigong (jing gong) is done by focusing on the inner movement of the breath and being in a still position.

When performed as a moving type of meditation, Qigong involves slow movements, mental focus, and deep diaphragmatic breathing. While doing this, you will be seeing chi flowing through your body in your mind's eye.

When doing this type of Qigong, your movements need to be fluid, often carefully choreographed, and must be synchronized with your breathing and awareness. Many of the best examples of these types of movements can be found in the following Chinese practices:

1. Tai Chi

2. Baguazhang

3. Xing Yi Quan

4. Wu Qin Xi Qigong, also known as The Five Animals Movements

As a kind of gentle physical exercise, you'll perform repeated movements that can help strengthen and stretch your body, increase fluid circulation in your body, improve proprioception and balance, and improve your awareness of how you move through space.

Passive Qigong

When you perform passive Qigong, you must hold certain postures for extended periods of time. To an extent, static Qigong resembles yoga. Examples of static postures are the Chinese martial art called Yiquan, which is based on Xingyiquan that puts a premium on static stance exercises. Another good example is the eight pieces of brocade or Baduanjin Qigong. This particular form of healing also involves a series of static postures.

You may also perform passive Qigong through breathing meditation, which uses breathing awareness, mantras, visualization, sounds, chants, and emphasis on Chinese philosophical concepts like moral values, aesthetics, and qi circulation. Meditative Qigong practices are used in a variety of ways. These include:

1. Balancing of qi flow throughout the body's pathways, including the meridian and cultivation of chi in the body's Dantian energy centers, As used in Taoist and traditional Chinese medical practices

2. Stilling the mind via outward focus an object or place or through internal focus using a mantra, emptiness, the breath, or a koan as part of Buddhist traditions

3. Self-enlightenment by focusing on virtues and humanity, as used in Confucian scholar traditions

Using Outside Objects

You may also practice Qigong using external objects such as eating herbs, getting a massage, interacting with other living things, and physical manipulation. In Daoist practice, for example, you may consume customized drinks and food for medical purposes. With martial arts, you can use body manipulation and massage as a way of using Qigong. You may also benefit from interactions with a Qigong professional specializing in transmitting healing Qigong to other people.

Internal Vs. External

Qigong can also be classified into two different systems from a health and therapy perspective: internal and external. Internal Qigong primarily focuses on self-cultivation and care, while external Qigong involves a professional therapist that transmits or directs Qi to the person, similar to reiki.

Qigong Forms

There are up to 75 forms of Qigong in ancient Chinese literature, while there are up to 56 contemporary forms you can find in a Qigong compendium, many of which were developed by people who have experienced healing through the practice. Generally, all these forms may be classified into five categories:

1. Medical

2. Martial Arts

3. Spiritual

4. Intellectual

5. Life Nourishment

Regardless of if you practice Qigong for health, exercise, or any other reason, it will involve most, if not all, of the following: intentional movement, rhythmic breathing, awareness, visualization, and sound (chanting). Other important aspects of effective Qigong practice include softness of the face (stoic expression), a solid stance (straight spine and firm footing), relaxed muscles and slightly bent joints, and balance/counterbalance of motion over your center of gravity. Some key objectives you'll focus on every session include equanimity, tranquility, and stillness. At the most advanced level, you'll hardly need to move while practicing Qigong.

The Three Qigong Treasures

If you reflect on your life so far, you'll likely remember experiencing a wide variety of emotions. There were times you probably felt euphoric, like you're on top of the world, while in other times, you may have felt like your entire world has crumbled and felt hopeless. You felt such emotions according to your internal state.

When you regularly practice Qigong, you'll be able to achieve optimal physical state through stabilizing your internal resources and life energy replenishment. The process by which you can achieve this is called energy healing.

Speaking of internal resources, practicing Qigong requires three specific ones: jing (essence), qi (energy), and shen (spirit). Called the three treasures of Qigong, these three terms form the key physiological functions of any living being. Therefore, these are crucial for sustaining life.

Qi

This refers to the energy that activates and mobilizes all of our body's structures and procedures. You get qi from various external sources, mostly the food and drinks you consume, the air you breathe, and your surrounding environment. The blood flowing through your veins is led by qi.

Experts consider it the halfway point of the other treasures, i.e., the gate through which passage to and from the body and spirit is possible. Essential for emotional balance and optimum physical health, a strong qi is evident in the ability to express oneself creatively and boldly.

Jing

Jing is qi in stored form, just like body fat is stockpiled. This is the equivalent of calories in the body that are kept for future use. As such, jing is the densest kind of energy among the three and is the one that's most important to your physical body. When you need energy, your body can draw from stored jing and transport it through your body's multiple energy channels. It is the foundation for your body's maturation, growth, and development over time.

Shen

As the final treasure, this resource or energy pertains to your ability to be self-aware and cognizant. Shen is linked closely to your spirit's energy and your behavior and mental health. Many Chinese medical experts have observed that people can lift or brighten their spirits through proper knowledge of their health.

What are the signs that your shen may be dull? These include:

1. Feeling anxious

2. Depression

3. Lethargy

4. Speaking voice that is soft or weak

5. Slurred speech

6. Inappropriate or weird behavior

These symptoms start to appear or become very apparent when the two other treasures can't provide adequate support.

On the other hand, you can tell that your shen is bright when the following are evident:

1. Eyes that are clear and alert

2. Coherent thoughts

3. A deep sense of joy and contentment

4. Speaking confidently and fluently

The Connection Between Your Purpose and the Three Treasures

As their collective name suggests, these three internal resources are crucial for your physical, emotional, and mental well-being, and as such, you must guard them and take care of them very carefully like you would physical treasures. Essentially, these three comprise who you are as a person and help you answer three important life questions:

1. Who are you?

2. Why are you here?

3. What do you want?

Your answers to these three questions are closely linked, much like how intimately related the three treasures are inside your own body.

Daily living eventually leads to weaker connections between your body, spirit, and mind. The greater the disconnections are, the more disconnected you'll feel from your life's purpose. When this becomes chronic, you eventually feel low in energy, lethargic, and unmotivated. Most of the time, your mind's thoughts aren't aligned with your spiritual path. It's pretty much like how you develop unhealthy habits despite knowing they're bad for you. That's why self-defeating or self-destructive actions may be indicative of the disintegration of your qi, jing, and shen.

Qigong's Interaction With Your Three Treasures

Regularly practicing Qigong can help you experience several benefits. The most important one is stabilizing your body, mind, and spirit. For you to experience optimal health and vitality, balance in all areas of your life is crucial. The more you're able to achieve this, the more vitality and harmony you'll experience in your life. On the other hand, you're likely to experience emotional turmoil and physical sickness when you live a chronically imbalanced life.

By regularly practicing Qigong, you'll be able to utilize the three treasures and live a harmonious and aligned life. This is because the practice allows you to integrate your qi, jing, and shen, which helps you achieve greater balance in all key areas of your life, particularly your mind, body, and spirit. When this happens, you'll be able to access your true purpose's highest expression.

Qigong starts to work in your life by helping you become more and more aware of all aspects of yourself, which allows you to gain a deep understanding of who you are. When you're able to do this, you can start strengthening your qi, optimize your jing levels, and ultimately, maximize your shen.

Uses of Qigong

You don't have to be a highly spiritual person, e.g., a monk, to practice Qigong. Like millions of people the world over engage in the practice for many reasons, so can you. A few of the most popular uses of Qigong include:

1. Cultivation of self

2. Exercise

3. Healing

4. Martial arts training

5. Meditation

6. Prevention of sickness is

7. Recreation

8. Relaxation

More than just a variety of uses, people from all walks of life can practice Qigong. From professional athletes to people with physical disabilities, Qigong is a popular form of activity because of its no-impact nature. It can be practiced in various positions, from lying down to standing up. This makes it a very practical form of physical exercise for a wide range of people with physical limitations, such as those recovering from injuries, dealing with disabilities, and are those who are older.

One of the most important uses of Qigong involves traditional Chinese medicine. Its practitioners, and those of integrative medicine and other forms of health practices, consider it a standard medical technique, and they frequently prescribe it for treatment of a myriad number of medical conditions such as

1. Back and leg discomfort

2. Cervical spondylosis

3. Chronic fatigue syndrome

4. Chronic liver conditions

5. Coronary artery disease

6. Diabetes

7. Hypertension

8. Insomnia

9. Menopause

10. Myopia

11. Obesity

12. Stomach ulcers

13. Tumors and cancers

And it's not just traditional Chinese medicine professionals that use Qigong for therapeutic purposes. Outside the U.S., many integrative medical practitioners use it to either supplement established scientific medical treatments. Several of its applications include promoting relaxation, developing fitness, rehabilitation of patients, and treating chronic conditions.

The reported efficacy of Qigong as a form of therapy may only be considered anecdotal. Clinical studies and systematic reviews reveal inadequate evidence for Qigong's efficacy as a medical treatment for specific conditions. It doesn't hurt to try to use it for such purposes. It's because Qigong is generally safe, with no adverse side effects observed during clinical trials across a diverse range of populations. Thus, its reputation as a safe medical practice.

Another reason why using Qigong for therapeutic purposes is its practicality. Using it for self-care and tails very minimal or no cost at all, and when administered as part of group care, its cost efficiency becomes even more glaring.

Qigong isn't completely risk-free. It has its share of associated cautions, too, even if minor or minimal. Things you'll need to exercise caution with as you start to get into it include possible sprains or muscle strains. You can minimize or completely avoid these by making a habit of stretching before Qigong. To minimize or eliminate any potential medical risks, you should first consult with your doctor before starting the practice.

Benefits of the Practice

Throughout the centuries, its practitioners have vouched for and the many benefits they experienced because of regular Qigong practice. These benefits can be generally classified as physiological and psychological.

Physiological Benefits

One of the key physiological benefits associated with the practice is higher bone density. Normally, this benefit is associated with exercises that involve lifting weights or working against resistance. Exercises that involve little or no resistance or weights can have the same effect.

In a 2006 study, researchers discovered that women who regularly perform Qigong for exercise experienced a significant increase in bone mineral density compared to those in a no-exercise control group. Considering that Qigong involves minimal or no resistance or weights, it was a pleasant surprise to find it can help increase bone density.

Another key physiological benefit of performing Qigong regularly is better pulmonary and cardiovascular function. This has been reported in studies like Qigong for Hypertension: A Systematic Review of Randomized Clinical Trials (Myeong Soo Lee[1], Max H Pittler, Ruoling Guo, Edzard Ernst, 2007), where subjects' blood pressures went down. The practice also shows potential in lowering heart rate and increasing its variability, both of which are very important health indicators.

You may also develop significantly better body balance when you regularly perform Qigong. One study found that patients who suffer from muscular dystrophy, healthy senior citizens, and women who live sedentary lifestyles improved their balance using Qigong.

To further strengthen your immune system, regularly practicing Qigong may also greatly benefit you. You see, studies have associated Qigong with several positive immune system responses. One of them is a 2004-published clinical trial entitled Assessment of Immunological Parameters Following a Qigong Training Program (Juan M Manzaneque, Francisca M Vera, Enrique F Maldonado, Gabriel Carranque, Victor M Cubero, Miguel Morell, Maria J Blanca). In the trial, researchers noted that subjects' multiple immune system blood markers improved significantly after one month of Qigong practice compared to just receiving their usual care. One such response is increased antibody levels after getting flu vaccinations for Qigong practitioners compared to those who aren't. Another observed response is significantly better regulation of the inflammation marker interleukin-6 in subjects that regularly practiced Qigong compared to those who didn't.

Finally, regularly practicing Qigong may improve somatic symptoms, which has been shown in various studies like Group and Home-Based Tai Chi in Elderly Subjects With Knee Osteoarthritis: A Randomized Controlled Trial (Brismee J-M, Paige RL, Chyu M-C, Boatright JD, Hagar JM, McCaleb JA, et al.) that was published in 2007. Somatic symptoms include physical discomforts such as pain, shortness of breath, and abdominal discomfort.

Psychological Benefits

It's not just your body that may benefit from this practice, but your mind and emotions too. One of Qigong's best psychological benefits is better life quality, which we can define as your perceived physical health, core beliefs, mental state, relationship with your environment, and social relationships. Several studies – such as the 2007-published study of Lee Y. K. Lee & Woo involving 139 residents of a health care facility - have shown that Qigong can help improve a person's quality of life compared to people who don't practice it.

You may also benefit from better self-efficacy if you practice Qigong regularly. We may define self-efficacy as your confidence in accomplishing things and overcome challenges. Studies like Impact of Qigong Exercise on Self-Efficacy and Other Cognitive Perceptual Variables in Patients with Essential Hypertension (Lee, Myung-Suk & Lim, Hyun-Ja & Lee, Myeong Soo. (2004) had shown that subjects who regularly performed Qigong experienced greater self-efficacy than their inactive control peers, particularly with their received ability to handle challenging or stressful situations.

Regularly performing chi gong may also lower your stress biomarkers or hormones like cortisol, epinephrine, and norepinephrine. Studies such as The Effects of Qigong on Reducing Stress and Anxiety and Enhancing Body–Mind Well-being by Yvonne WY Chow and Andrew MH Siu (2011) have shown lower levels of these stress hormones in subjects that regularly practiced Qigong compared to those that didn't.

Performing this regularly can help you minimize or reduce anxiety and depression if you are suffering from these. Based on depression scales utilized in several studies like the 2005-published randomized control trial (Randomized Controlled Trial of Qigong) in the Treatment of Mild Essential Hypertension (Cheung, Lo, Fong, Chan, Wong, Wong, Lam, Lau, and Karlberg (2005), Qigong helped decrease symptoms of depression in subjects who practiced it compared to those who didn't. Not only that, but it also appears that subjects who do Qigong regularly registered significantly lower anxiety levels compared to an active exercise group. Measurements were taken using the Self-Rating Anxiety Scale.

Scientific Studies on Qigong's Benefits

Compared to Tai chi, Qigong doesn't have as many high-quality research studies to conclusively support many of its reported benefits, most of which are anecdotal. To establish the practice has numerous benefits, more such research studies are needed.

But despite this, Qigong is still worth giving a shot. After all, it's a very safe practice that normally involves relaxation and very gentle movements, both of which are considered good for health in general. Also, practicing Qigong doesn't require spending money. Getting into it gives you opportunities to gain lots of benefits with minimal or no risk.

Still, several studies have documented Qigong-related benefits. One of them was a 2010 published study in the prestigious American Journal of Health Promotion, which reviewed 66 studies involving 6400 subjects. In A Comprehensive Review of Health Benefits of Qigong and Tai Chi, researchers Roger Jahnke, Linda K Larkey, Carol Elizabeth Rogers, and Jennifer Etnier found various positive results while combing through the studies. Specifically, they found that regular practice of Qigong and Tai chi helped improve the subjects' balance and bone health.

Another important study on Qigong's health benefits was Qigong for Hypertension: A Systematic Review of Randomized Clinical Trials by Myeong Soo Lee, Max H Pittler, Ruoling Guo, and Edzard Ernst. Published in the Journal of Hypertension in 2007, the researchers reported that regular Qigong exercise appeared to improve the subjects' blood pressures mildly, but the study's authors qualified that more study needs to be done to confirm their reported results.

Another study conducted in the same year, published in the Journal of Alternative and Complementary Medicine this time, reported another positive health benefit among its subjects: mild positive effects in diabetes control. In A Qualitative Review of the

Role of *Qigong* in the Management of Diabetes (Liu Xin, Yvette D. Miller, and Wendy J. Brown), the authors also issued a similar statement, i.e., more conclusive studies are needed to validate the benefits they reported.

To date, researchers continue to conduct studies on the health benefits of regular Qigong practice. These include the possibility of using Qigong as a complementary cancer treatment.

Chapter 2: Understanding Energy: Qi, Yin-Yang, Jing, and Shen

Qi may be defined as the energy the flows throughout our bodies, which provides us with the necessary minerals, nutrients, and circulation for holistic health. In traditional Chinese medicine, qi is believed to be a person's life force, and as such, it is the best way to gauge vitality.

As an ancient practice, Qigong has been used by doctors who specialize in holistic or integrative medicine and acupuncturists to help their patients restore their bodies to their natural and optimally healthy state. Such professionals also use it to help their clients achieve a Zen state.

The concept of qi isn't exclusive to ancient Chinese culture. In the Yogic or Ayurvedic tradition, this energy or life force is called prana, but people sometimes confuse chi with qi. So, which is which?

While they both refer to the same thing, many use one term over the other depending on the context of the discussion. In terms of restoring a person's balance, qi is the better term to use because it is the physical or nourishing aspect of the food we eat, the water we drink, and the air we breathe. Experts often use qis as their reference when referring to the vital fluids and the energy that circulates inside our bodies. Regardless, both have the same ultimate goal: helping you achieve optimal physical and mental health every day.

What makes qi very important for our health? It's what flows through our bodies via the meridians, and it is responsible for our blood circulation. When our blood and qi move throughout the body properly, we experience optimal health and harmony. In ancient Chinese culture, qi is considered as the energy derived from food and drinks, and a type of gas or pressure that promotes adequate movement inside our bodies.

If optimal health and balance are the byproducts of a balanced qi, the opposite indicates deficiencies in the same. You may develop qi deficiencies through any of the following, individually or in combination:

1. Dirty water

2. Lack of quality sleep

3. Polluted air

4. Poor diet

5. Lack of nutrients or other physical elements for optimal health and performance

Your qi may also become deficient when you don't stimulate your mind sufficiently, if you get insufficient love from others, and if you don't get enough social interactions.

How does qi deficiency manifest itself? Some signs include:

1. Chronic pain

2. Depression

3. Fatigue

4. Feeling chronically stressed

5. Frequent weakness of the muscles

6. Hormonal imbalances

7. Irritability

8. Lethargy

9. Regular cramping

It may be tempting to think the more, the merrier with your qi. Nothing can be further from the truth. For optimal health and wellbeing, balance is key. That is why it is also possible to have excess qi and fall short of optimal physical, mental, and emotional health.

What factors contribute to accumulating excess qi? The most common ones include:

1. Chronic stress

2. Environmental toxins such as air and water pollutants

3. Excess physical activity, i.e., chronic overexertion

4. Overeating

5. Toxic emotions

Balancing Your Qi

Fortunately, achieving the right qi levels isn't rocket science. You can choose from various mind-body practices and techniques, from Qigong and tai chi to reiki and massages. The simplest way to rebalance and keep your qi that way is to avoid over exhausting yourself and getting enough quality sleep regularly. Other practical ways to achieve and maintain your qi balance include acupuncture and movement-based hobbies that promote stretching of the muscles and improved blood flow throughout the body.

If you suffer from imbalanced qi, do your best to identify its reason instead of just trying to alleviate its symptoms. Imbalanced qi is caused by many factors, from dirty air and water to unhealthy food and chronic stress. That's why a healthy, balanced diet and getting adequate rest regularly are key to achieving and maintaining qi balance.

The Five Elements Framework

With Chinese culture, the five elements serve as important foundational pieces for many areas of people's lives. These elements are earth, water, air, fire, and metal. It's no surprise that the five elements framework also plays a crucial role in the Qigong practice, particularly in achieving balance for optimal health and wellbeing.

These five elements provide a comprehensive system of organizing all-natural phenomena in the world into major patterns or groups in nature. Each element falls into specific seasons, directions, climates, stages of life, internal organs, emotions, and many others that are important in our lives. The categories are practically limitless, and these five elements, as taught in Chinese culture, provide a thorough understanding of natural laws and universal order.

When you understand the five elements framework, you'll see the relationship between your body and nature and, more importantly, how the different dimensions of your relating to and affect each other. As you start studying or learning the five elements framework, you must focus on the fact this multi-dimensional perspective of life can provide you with a diagnostic template by which you can learn to spot imbalances in your body, emotions, mind, and spirit. The more you're able to do this, the easier it will be for you to correct any imbalances quickly before they worsen. This framework includes your key internal organs and their relationships with each other pertaining to optimal health and wellbeing.

The five elements of framework or theory can tell you a lot about the environment you're in. For one, it can show you how all things are connected. Let's take water, for example.

According to ancient Chinese culture, water is related to several things, including fear, the kidneys, the color black, winter, cold climates, and the north. During winters, the environmental essence is cold, which impacts and is related to the kidney in several ways. Fear is also linked to cold and the kidneys, albeit in subtle and inconspicuous ways at times.

Air, water, earth, fire, and metal also show you your body's systems and structures and how they relate to each other. These can show you how you are connected to your environment and the natural world at large and how the world is part of the entire universe. While many people these days have severed their connection to nature, the universal idea of interconnection remains valid, nonetheless.

Balance

You may consider the five elements as the basic energies of mother nature in motion. They aren't static, but rather dynamic relationships exist between them all. The two fundamental relationships that govern them our generation and support. Unless these two are balanced, it may be very hard or even impossible to achieve optimal health and wellbeing.

What does generation mean? This refers to a relationship that results in continuous growth. A good picture of the generation is that of a mother and a child. After giving birth, the mother provides her baby with nutrients through her breast milk and other external resources, ensuring her child's survival and growth. This type of relationship can be seen between the liver and kidneys, where the kidney helps generate the liver.

And when we talk about support in the context of the five elements, we talk about a specific type of relationship - one that helps restrict or restrain that energy or force of the others to ensure growth at the right pace. Growing too fast or too slow, too strong or too weak, can lead to major imbalances that can hinder you from achieving optimal health and wellbeing.

Types of Qi

Inside your body, there are two general types or classifications of qi: pre-natal and post-natal.

Pre-Natal Qi

Also called the "source qi," it refers to the vital energy that both parents give to their babies at birth. You may think of it as a person's essence or basic matter, which is the native force supporting the body's tissues and organs. This energy is directly linked to the primary, and most important energy center in the human body called the Ming Men and the body's Eight Extraordinary Vessels.

Post-Natal Qi

On the other hand, this type of energy is a combination of qi you can get from the food and drinks you consume and the air you breathe. It's directly linked to the 12 primary organ systems or meridians of your body. When combined with the pre-natal qi, they create your body's true qi, i.e., the source of energy you use in daily living.

Impact of Qigong

The primary reasons for developing Qigong are balancing, enhancing, and harmonizing the true qi for optimal health, longevity, and spiritual development. Regularly practicing Qigong can lead to direct and positive impacts on the key factors that affect your health and wellbeing: pre-natal qi, post-natal qi, essence, and spirit. These work together and can help oversee your life activities and connect you to the divine.

The Yin and the Yang

One of the most popular concepts in Chinese culture, these two represent the two foundational aspects of all things that exist. Interdependent and complementary, you may think of yin and yang as the foundational relationships the run through everything. When one or both of these are imbalanced, you may suffer from illnesses because you can experience health and well-being when yin and yang are balanced.

The best way to describe the properties of these two is those of fire and water. Yin refers to water, and yang refers to fire. Several qualities that best describe the yin are those that can be said of water:

1. Cold
2. Contracting
3. Dim
4. Fall season
5. Internal
6. Night
7. Thinking
8. Winter season

In relation to your body, it is the bottom, front, right side, and interior parts. The viscera is your inside yin while the earth is your outside one.

But the qualities that can best describe young are those related to fire, such as

1. Bright

2. Daytime

3. Expanding

4. External

5. Hot

6. Rising

7. Spring season

8. Summer season

As it relates to your body, the yang relates to the top, back, left side, and outside. Your bubbles may be considered your inside yang, while heaven is your outside yang.

Being closely connected and interdependent, yin and yang can affect each other when imbalanced. They are deeply involved in all aspects of your life, and to enjoy optimal health and well-being, both must be in a state of balance. Sickness can result from an imbalance in either or both. Once the two have become completely separated, death is the result.

Jing (Body Energy)

Being one of the three treasures of Qigong, jing has no direct translation in the English language. The best English definition often used to describe this treasure is "essence." This is because jing is what really comprises a person, including you, even before your birth.

Many people consider jing as DNA. This is because as DNA's double-strand helix genetic blueprints determine your physiological and energy characteristics before birth, jing does the same as the essence or substance that makes up who you are.

In ancient traditional Chinese medicine philosophy, people believe that all people have a set amount of jing when they're born. Healthy babies have their entire lives to manage the jing they're born with, just like how people budget their inheritance or savings upon retirement. Basically, jing goes inside the body and permanently anchors all the energy people will need throughout their lives.

Now, you may be wondering: why should you bother about caring for your jing when you basically can do nothing about it, given you just inherit it? In other words, why even bother learning about and managing it if you have no say as to the amount you get upon birth?

Now that is a good question! And the answer is simple: doing so can help you "budget" you're jing such that you can live the longest and healthiest life possible. If you spend too much of it as you would with overspending your money, it will quickly run out, and when this happens, your life is over as you know it.

To be able to effectively "budget" or manage your jing supply, you must know the things that can drain it. A few ways that your essence can leak from your body include:

1. A highly stressful lifestyle

2. Being frequently angry

3. Chronic sleep deprivation

4. Substance abuse

5. Too much ejaculation

More than just being aware of what can cause your jinx to leak excessively from your body, you also have to recognize when it is happening. Several of the most common red flags indicative of excessive jing-leaking include:

1. Chronic inability to focus

2. Feeling and looking tired throughout the day

3. Feeling that you're living life without purpose

4. Hair loss

5. You look older than you are or premature aging

In theory, your immune system may be compromised when your jing is wasted or is leaking excessively. This means you can be more vulnerable to sicknesses and diseases. If you're able to care for and manage your jing wisely, you'll be able to boost your immune system, and your body won't easily fall prey to flu, colds, allergies, and the like.

And lastly, you also need to learn how to preserve or even replenish your essence to live the longest and healthiest life possible. One of the best ways you can do these is by eating the right foods, which include:

1. Bee pollen

2. Black rice

3. Bone broth

4. Internal organ meats

5. Kidney beans

6. Poultry and fish eggs

7. Royal jelly

8. See vegetables

9. Seeds

You may also use Chinese herbs that may help replenish your essence. These include mulberry, goji berry, he shou wu, and shan yao. Other ways you can preserve or replenish your jing include:

1. Acupuncture

2. Engaging in regular qi-building exercises like Qigong and tai chi

3. Minimizing sexual intercourse or masturbation

4. Regular meditation

Your Jing, Blood, and Kidneys

One of the worst things you can do for your jing is eating a standard American diet known as SAD. There is a good reason it's called sad!

Today, the average American diet is too high on junk and processed foods, so major illnesses and conditions such as heart problems and cancers are becoming even more prevalent among the population. Coupled with a lack of regular exercise and chronic high-stress levels, these can wreak havoc on any person's jing.

Now, how is jing related to your blood? Excessive jing leaking due to poor diet, sedentary lifestyles, and chronic stress can negatively affect your body's ability to produce blood. Based on ancient traditional Chinese medicine theories, the jing is stored in a person's kidneys, from which it travels to the bone and ultimately becoming bone marrows. As we all know, blood is produced in the bone marrow.

And speaking of chronic stress as one of the critical jing-leaking factors, how does it contribute to the leaking? For this, it's important to understand a theory called the adrenal fatigue theory.

In western functional medicine, it is believed that adrenal fatigue is caused by chronic excess cortisol levels, which is a stress hormone. In turn, cortisol tends to flood the body when under chronically high levels of stress. When this happens, a person's hormonal, metabolic pathways are both diverted and disrupted in response to the need to produce more cortisol.

Now here's the interesting part: cortisol is produced by the adrenal glands, which coincidentally rests on top of the kidneys. If the adrenal glands are overworked, it also negatively affects the kidneys, in which jing is stored. This is why chronically excessive stress levels can lead to excessive leaking of the jing via wreaking havoc on the kidneys.

Your Essence and Your Brain

Excessively leaking jing isn't just bad for your kidneys and blood. It can also negatively affect your brain.

Based on traditional Chinese medicine, your brain contains a sea of marrow, and if too much essence is leaking from you, your kidneys become weak and eventually lead to malnourishment of your brain. When this happens, telltale signs include the inability to concentrate, poor memory, brain fog, and confusion.

Working Together With Your Qi and Shen

Inside your body, jing is the densest physical matter, and it determines who and what you are, just like DNA. Based on traditional Chinese medicine, your essence nourishes, cools, and fuels your body. When you live a moderate or healthy lifestyle, which includes getting enough rest, a healthy diet, and adequate stress management, you don't just help preserve or replenish your jing but also support your qi.

And when you're able to manage and contain your essence without excessive leaks properly, you enjoy abundant levels of qi. When both of these are optimal, you may expect your spirit or your shen to be optimal.

And speaking of which...

Shen (Spiritual Energy)

The last of the three treasures of Qigong refers to the energy of your heart. In traditional Chinese medicine, this is represented by the fire element. As a form of energy, your shen directly connects with those of your spleen and livers.

Your qi relates to your vital energy and breath, both of which animate you as a person. But your jing is the energy you get from the foods and drinks you consume and the air you breathe, both of which constitute your physical essence. How is your shen related to your qi and jing? Your shen comes from the latter two, and in turn, it gives energy to your qi.

Sources of Shen

Your shen energy has two sources: pre-natal and post-natal. Your pre-natal shen, as the term implies, is that which you were born with. Your energy connects with the internal aspect of the universe, also called the Tao. When you're familiar with or know the concept of shen, you'll be able to connect with what it's called in TCM as the mind of the Tao or of the universe. This is permanent and may be considered as your eternal soul, but you may find it difficult to recognize because of how your mind has been conditioned from childhood.

As the name implies, too, post-natal shen is that which you're able to derive or acquire after being born. Where do you get this? Your jing and qi.

Your post-natal shen can be directly shaped or influenced by the environment in which you live, the habits you develop, and mental conditioning. Basically, it's directly formed by your external environment and your own thoughts and behaviors. Speaking of thoughts, chronic overthinking, as with any excessive behavior, may prematurely exhaust your shen or even lead to disconnection from your pre-natal one.

The Five Elements and Your Shen

All five organs are responsible for containing (or *housing*) your shen. Your heart is the primary container; all of your other internal organs, including their related energies, can affect your shen. It's because every organ in your body contains a part or area of your being, which in turn can impact your physical, mental, and spiritual wellbeing. This is why in traditional Chinese medicine, balancing the body's energies is crucial, non-negotiable even, for optimal health and wellbeing, both physical and spiritual.

Because your shen is the energy of your heart, it helps you achieve a healthy balance between your mind and your emotions. Your emotions can help regulate your reasoning and vice versa. To a great extent, you'd be right to assume that it helps you manage your consciousness.

Your shen may also be the path to your spirit, which sets you apart from animals. When you're able to balance your shen regularly, it'll be natural for you to follow the rhythms of the universe and the laws of nature. A healthy and balanced shen means a joy-filled life.

On the other hand, excessive and uncontrollable emotions may lead to an unbalanced shen. If you cannot handle them, the challenges in your life may lead to nervous tension, sleeplessness, and anxiety. Some ways you can tell if this is already happening is a profound and chronic sense of sadness, restlessness, and chronic fatigue.

Balancing Your Shen

If you find yourself disconnected from your post-natal shen or the mind of the Tao, one way you can reconnect with it is through regular meditation. You can also reconnect with your tranquil and empowering inner space by getting regular sleep and through centered prayers.

Externally, you may utilize specific herbs to balance your shen. These include reishi mushrooms and gotu kola, but before supplementing your daily regimen with such herbs, first consult with a professional herbalist or a medical professional. This is especially important if preexisting medical conditions require maintenance medications or if you're pregnant or nursing.

Chapter 3: The Three Intentful Corrections: Body, Breath, and Mind

One of the most important things you must know about the practice of Qigong is the foundational concept of the three *intentful* corrections. In particular, these refer to important corrections that need to be made about your body, the way you breathe, and mental focus or mind. These corrections need to be made because any imbalances in these key areas can keep you from optimizing the benefits of the practice.

Fortunately, these three intentful corrections aren't difficult. You need not be very strict about following them because they are more focused on paying close attention to your body and doing your best to live as healthy as possible.

Your Body

When it comes to your body, the corrections pertain to your posture. This, together with routing and stances, are crucial for ensuring the balanced circulation of your qi. When your posture isn't correct, the flow of your qi can be disrupted.

When you start practicing Qigong, you will assume stationary and moving postures. Regardless of if you are standing up or sitting down, you'd want to be as tall and straight as possible. Doing this helps give your organs more working room and enable your bones to hold you up more easily. When you stand up or sit down straight, your spine's bones can stack perfectly on top of each other to provide maximum support for your body. Whenever you slouch, most of the work to keep you from tipping over goes to your muscles. This can either fatigue you more quickly, lead to muscle strain and tightness, or both.

One thing to consider so you always be conscious of assuming a straight and upward position, whether sitting down or standing up, is that the head is heavy. The inability to maintain a straight and upward posture can cause a forward-positioned head, which is common among senior citizens. When you bring your head up and slightly back, you may relieve your neck and shoulders of the strain of having to hold it up.

Sitting in a slouched position has other disadvantages, too. In such a position, you tend to pack or compress your organs together. When this happens, you may impede their optimal function. Blood and other body fluid circulation may also be limited when your organs are compressed together. When you sit with good posture, you're not just able to optimize organ functions and bodily fluid circulation; you may strengthen your weak core muscles, too. So, sitting up properly, i.e., in a straight and upright posture, can help make your body stronger too. This is even more important because most of the time, you're just sitting down.

Now, let's talk about standing up. Most people tend to stand with their pelvises tilted too far forward. Especially in senior citizens, this creates a "swayback," which isn't healthy for the lower back. An easy way to restore the pelvis back into a neutral position is by imagining your tailbone being pulled down by a weight. This helps you create a pelvic ball that can properly hold your digestive organs, help you become more stable and grounded, and even look thinner.

Another important posture you must learn when exercising Qigong is to avoid pulling yourself up using your shoulders or chest. The proper posture should be having the shoulders always relaxed, hanging down, and slightly drawn back. An easy way to do this is to imagine a string tied to the top of your head and being pulled upward. This helps you stretch and lengthen your spine, which can help you look thinner, even taller. More importantly, it decompresses your internal organs and gives them more room to work optimally.

Your joints also play an important role in assuming proper posture in Qigong. In particular, you must keep your joints soft and bent slightly when performing the exercise. They should neither be tight nor locked.

With your arms, they should be shaped like a bow. As far as your legs go, they should be slightly bent at the knees. If your leg and core muscles aren't strong enough yet, you may need more time to practice these and strengthen them. The best way to strengthen these muscles is to simply use them the way nature designed them to be used: with good posture and gentle movements.

Speaking of movements, they're slow and flowing when doing Qigong. More than just being easy on your joints, slow movements also help strengthen your muscles. In particular, your arm and leg muscles need to work against gravity when slowly lifting and bringing down the arm and upper body, respectively. Because of the slow movements, it's like you're performing resistance or lifting exercises using your body weight. Hence, performing Qigong correctly may help strengthen your upper and lower bodies, as well as your core muscles, without straining your joints.

But the flowing, repetitive nature of the movements can help you learn to relax better by activating your parasympathetic nervous system. This is because a few of the movements involved are like rocking ourselves to sleep. So more than just strength and flexibility benefits, Qigong can help you lower your stress and even facilitate healing in several areas of your health. To that extent, the overall impact of exercise on your health and wellbeing is more important than the practice itself.

When performing Qigong movements, consider these basic guidelines:

1. Each exercise provides numerous options, from sitting down to walking, which helps you do Qigong in ways that are most appropriate for your current physical fitness level.

2. If you are assisting others, don't grab them by their wrist but instead offer your hands.

3. Keep your range of movements within your comfort zone and avoid overstretching because pain isn't necessary to enjoy the practice's benefits.

4. The practice's primary goal is relaxation, so always try to have fun and relax instead of stressing over the movements.

5. You don't have to be rigid or strict about the exercises, and you can modify them according to your specific needs or conditions.

6. You don't have to perform exercises perfectly to enjoy their benefits because the important thing is to continue doing something rather than nothing.

Your Breathing

You may be wondering, is there actually a right way of breathing and, by extension, a wrong way of doing it? If you're alive, doesn't that mean you're breathing the right way already?

To clarify, the second intentful correction, your breathing, doesn't mean the way you're breathing is wrong. Otherwise, you wouldn't get enough oxygen and die of asphyxiation eventually.

What is meant by correcting your breathing is working on how you breathe to maximize both the quantity and quality of air that goes into your body. In short, it's a transition from sub-optimal breathing to an optimal one.

So, what does sub-optimal breathing look like? The simplest way to describe it is chest breathing, where a person uses muscles between the ribs to suck air into the lungs' upper regions. This breathing type may be considered relatively shallow because it only fills the upper part of the lungs with air, failing to maximize their full capacities.

In Qigong, you'll learn to transition from chest breathing to belly breathing. This type of breathing involves slow and deep breaths that fill your entire lungs from the bottom up. This is the optimal form and intentful correction of the breath.

If you are used to just breathing, you'll immediately feel the difference when you start to take deep and slow belly breaths. Researchers have noted that as few as ten deep and slow belly breaths a day can help you achieve a 10 to 30% improvement in vitality and physical endurance. If as simple as ten of these can help you significantly change how you feel and, in your energy, can you imagine if you make this your normal breathing habit?

Deep belly breaths can help you relax so much better and much faster. Scientifically speaking, breathing this way helps slow down the heart rate. This is why people are often instructed to take slow and deep breaths whenever they feel anxious or nervous. It isn't a coincidence that one of the physical symptoms of anxiety, stress, and nervousness is shallow and rapid breaths, usually via the chest.

Ideally, you should use your diaphragm muscles to generate the necessary pressure for drawing oxygen into your lungs. When you take a deep breath, your torso expands in six different directions simultaneously. As you do this, your body's pressure change helps move the lymph and other bodily fluids through your tissues. Your internal organs experience a delicate rolling motion massage every time you breathe deeply through your belly. These are some of their reasons deep belly breaths are very helpful to heal the body on many levels.

And another way of breathing that can help you release emotional tension is moans and sighs. The Qigong exercise call "lazy monkey wakes up" uses moaning or sighing to release tension from the body. This exercise also uses the sound "ha" as a toning form for breaking up stagnation and congestion in the chest area. Another popular way of breathing that helps release tension, specifically from the shoulders, is laughing.

Another way that slow and deep belly breaths help you relax is by calming your mind. Remember how people tend to breathe fast and shallowly when very stressed and nervous? By slowing down and deepening your breaths, you'll be able to hit two birds with one stone: deeper breaths and slower heart rate. Together, these can help you alleviate stress and anxiety symptoms and, ultimately, calm your mind. As an ancient eastern saying goes, "the mind rides on the breath as a rider does on a horse." This is why you need to learn to control your breathing. Doing so also helps you control your mind.

Your Mind

Your mind, specifically mental focus, is the final intentful correction that needs to be addressed for optimal Qigong practice. The best mindset you can have to get the most out of the exercise is to be present, centered, and always aware of when your mind strays away from the moment.

Let's face it, most of us tend to spend much of our days either thinking about the past or worrying about the future. Not that these are bad but overdoing them can prevent optimal health and wellbeing. It's all right to think of these things now and then, but if they occupy our mind most of the time, it's neither healthy nor productive. That is why in Qigong, it is important to be continuously aware of focusing on the present moment.

When you shift your focus to the present moment during Qigong, you can let old grudges go and set aside anxieties and fears, even if only for the moment. Because you need to focus on gentle movements and proper breathing while performing Qigong, you'll be able to train your mind to focus on the present moment and let go of past and future concerns. More importantly, your ability to do so can help you experience the joys and peace of the moment.

For most people, their attention is fixed on what's happening in their external environment. Chances are, they're always on the lookout for incoming "attacks" on them, such as criticisms, mistakes, unhappiness, blame, and even finding that one person who will complete them. If this is you, you can find solace in the fact that Qigong can help you regain your inner balance by shifting your focus inside you instead of outside. By focusing your attention on your breaths and movements, you can train your mind to focus on the present much better and ultimately achieve balance.

Especially for people living in the United States or other western countries, over-analysis seems to be a common habit. Many troublesome thoughts run through their heads and rob them of their joy, such as

1. Am I ever going to find the one true love that will make me complete?

2. Do I look fat in this shirt?

3. What are the chances I'll fail in this endeavor?

4. When will I ever achieve financial abundance?

5. Why the hell did I even think about doing that?

In Qigong, you'll be encouraged to bring your mental awareness or focus back to your chest area, where the heart center or the heart-mind resides. When you're able to do this regularly, you'll be able to harness fresh mental resources for solving problems as they arise. This is only possible when you're able to slow down the needless mental chatter in your mind. Regularly practicing Qigong is an excellent way of achieving this.

When it comes to intently correcting your mind or focus, grounding is very important. This refers to being connected to the earth. Learning to focus on the moment can help you go outside of your head and become increasingly aware not just of your body and its movements but also of its connection to the planet.

Think about it: why does walking in nature trails or hiking in the mountains feel so relaxing and invigorating? It's because these are a few of the most effective ways of connecting with the earth, a.k.a., grounding. Through regular Qigong practice, you'll be able to achieve the same connection to the earth. How?

According to traditional Chinese medicine, you can do this by focusing on how your pelvis is currently tilted. When you're able to achieve the right pelvic tilt, you'll also be able to open up your groin area. When these happen, your legs start to feel more connected to the flow of your body and its movements and, eventually, establish a genuine connection with nature.

When you're able to focus your mind on the present moment, you'll be able to notice everything within and around you. Then, you'll be able to enjoy the now and feel one with the earth.

Movement Principles

As mentioned earlier, the movements involved in Qigong are easy, smooth, flowing, very deliberate, and slow. You must always remember not the overdo the movements to avoid straining or injuring muscles or joints. Again, the emphasis is on movement within your physical comfort zone with just enough stretch, which should never feel painful.

As with the movements, breathe deeply, smoothly, and deeply. Your breathing must also be coordinated with your movements. With movement and breathing coordination, the general principle is to breathe in as you relax your muscles and breathe out as you contract them or as you lower your body.

Mentally speaking, you must focus on the moment by paying close attention to how you execute your movements and coordinating it with your breathing. This is one crucial aspect that differentiates Qigong from other forms of exercise. As long as you do this, you'll be able to keep your mind centered on the moment. Eventually, your focus will be directed inwardly so you can be keenly aware of what's going on in your body.

Deep and slow breathing. Repeatedly performing slow and flowing movements. Meditative focus. Together, these three elements synergistically stimulate your body's relaxation response as a means of reversing the negative effects of aging, stress, and promoting healing.

Chapter 4: Standing Qigong: Stances, Posture, and Balance

Now, we are ready to talk about how to practice Qigong. In this chapter, you will learn the basics of performing standing Qigong, specifically stances, posture, and balance.

Warming Up

As with any type of physical exercise, warming up is highly recommended. While Qigong isn't as strenuous or impactful as most other types of exercises, it still involves movements that stretch your muscles and joints. Without proper warmup, you increase your risks for overstretching or straining. Here's how you can start warming up for every session:

1. Warm up by performing ankle circles. Follow them up with nice circles and, finally, hip circles. Do at least nine circles each to warm up properly.

2. Next, warm and loosen up your shoulders. Do this by rolling your shoulders up, back, and down for at least eight repetitions. Follow it up with rolling the same up, forward, and down for at least eight reps, too.

3. Then, move on to your neck. Gently roll it clockwise and reverse the movement by rolling it counterclockwise after one repetition or one full round. To roll it, start by dropping your head forward, then rolling it gently to your right, to the back (your face should be facing upward at this point), to the left, and stopping when it returns to your starting point. Reverse the movement to perform a counterclockwise roll.

4. Finally, warm up your arms. Begin by putting your right hand behind your right shoulder as you breathe in. Your right elbow should be pointing upward and forming a peak at this point.

5. While holding your breath, put your left hand on the right elbow.

6. As you breathe out, gently push down your right elbow to slide your right hand as far down your back as comfortably possible for a light stretch. As you release the push, breathe in again. Do this at least two more times before switching to the other arm for at least three repetitions.

When you're done with the warmup, you may now perform the exercise.

Postures

One of the most enduring forms of Qigong, one that has withstood the test of time, involves standing in a wide variety of postures. Most Qigong practitioners continue doing these because it's believed to be a very effective way to improve one's energy and health. It's not just limited to those. Some traditional forms of Chinese martial arts also incorporate specific standing Qigong postures for developing strength and power.

In Qigong, the standing postures used aren't just based on a thorough understanding of the physical body but also of the life force energy that animates every living thing on earth, i.e., the qi.

With good standing postures, relaxation is important because when both mind and body are relaxed, qi can flow optimally throughout the body.

Standing Qigong postures are often thought of as the naturally fluid model of the human body because of their natural focus on fluidity or flow of movements and relaxation. Once you start assuming these standing postures, you'll be able to tell how different they are from what we know to be as "good posture" today - shoulders pulled back, just lifted up, legs straight, and the chin raised.

Two important principles involved in Qigong are balance and relaxation. When you're able to balance your body through natural alignment, you need minimum muscular tension just to be able to maintain an upright standing position. This helps minimize or greatly reduce muscular fatigue and strain, allowing you to perform Qigong more efficiently.

For learning proper Qigong posture, you must understand that it's not something you'll be able to do instantly. It's because you probably developed sub-optimal postural habits from the time you were a child until adulthood. Given these habits took time to develop, you may also take time to relearn a natural and optimal posture. So, you shouldn't be rushing it, but instead, understand and accept that the Qigong way of doing this is to peel away accumulated postural habits one at a time, layer by layer.

Another important thing you must learn about proper Qigong posture is the 70% principle. This means you shouldn't force your body to do something beyond its current capacity, but instead, use no more than up to 70% of its capacity.

Remember that just as with anything worth doing or achieving, learning how to strike the proper standing postures in Qigong will require time and practice. If you go beyond your body's 70% capacity or worse, go beyond 100%, you won't achieve relaxation during the practice, and worse, you may injure yourself through things like overstretching.

Remember, take your time and always be cognizant that relaxation is a key factor or component of the practice.

Basic Standing Posture Alignments

These alignments start with your feet, as they are the foundation for any standing postures. Also, you may use them every day if you think they can be beneficial for you.

Feet Apart

Begin by standing with both feet about hip or shoulder-width apart. This means your feet must be beneath either your shoulders or your hips in this position.

The primary reason for this posture or alignment is to let your leg bones line up so that your muscles can be as relaxed as possible when you lower your body to the ground. If you try a much wider stance, you risk putting more work or tension on your muscles as you lower your body closer to the ground.

Parallel Feet

Bring your feet as close auras parallel to each other as comfortably possible. If your usual standing position has your feet turned in or out, it may take you a while to learn and adjust to this new stance. The important thing here is not to force and rush your feet in positions either strenuous or painful. Doing so only puts you at risk for injuries to your feet, hips, knees, or other body parts. So, always remember the 70% rule and proceed gradually.

Knees Slightly Bent

Instead of keeping your knees locked while standing, keep them slightly bent such that you can bounce your body up and down gently, such that your knee joints feel springy instead of rigid. Be careful not to bend the knees too much because doing so run you the risk of pushing your knees forward, which may transfer a lot of your body weight to your leg muscles. But locking your knee joints deprives them of "springiness," which is important for reducing or eliminating much of the impact or strain from them.

Lengthened Spine

Gently elevate the top of your head to "stretch" both your neck and your spine. If you are unfamiliar with how this is done, just imagine somebody gently lifting your head up by pulling on both your ears. Another way you can do this is by putting your thumbs beneath your skull, just under your ears, and lightly push your head up to elongate your spine.

Remember, the operative word here is "gently." If you push or pull too hard, you may tense your muscles such that relaxation, which is one of the important guiding principles of Qigong, becomes impossible.

Chin Slightly Sunk

Contrary to the modern perception of excellent posture, you must be cognizant not to lift your chin to appear taller. It's because doing so reduces the length of your nape, which may excessively curve your cervical spine. Remember that while lengthening the back of the neck is important, it shouldn't be at the expense of a curved spine.

Broad and Relaxed Shoulders

Instead of pulling your shoulders all the way back, allow them to naturally broaden sideward or outward. To do this, let them relax as much as possible and let gravity pull them down naturally. Next, gently broaden them from your sternum and spine to the tips of your shoulders.

If you follow your shoulder girdle's natural shape, your shoulders will broaden in a slightly concave manner instead of a straight line. To achieve the length you're after, follow your body's natural curves. Take note: this isn't the same as rounding your shoulders by collapsing it forward, like what you see with most people we have been working in front of their computers all day.

Empty Chest

In ancient tai chi tradition, there's a saying that goes like this: the spine lifts, and the chest empties into the belly. So, allow your chest to sink a little and stay soft instead of lifting it and letting it stick out. Just remember that the keyword phrase here is "sink a little" and not "collapse." You'll know if you're doing it right if this feels light.

This is encouraged for several good reasons, but the most important one is to relax your chest enough such that your qi can circulate efficiently down to the front of your body. This is because, based on ancient traditional Chinese medicine, stress and anxiety result from energy rising up to the front of a person's body and, in the process, getting stuck inside the chest and the head. Together with broadening your shoulders, thinking your chest slightly allows the back of your lungs to have more space to move when you breathe and facilitate efficient circulation of your energy down to the front of your body.

Let Go of the Pelvis

Last, let gravity sink your pelvis' big and heavy bones. When we talk about letting go of the pelvis, we're not talking about positioning your pelvis in a certain way. It's more about relaxing or releasing the muscles that hold it in position. Instead of tilting or tucking your pelvis, you'll be able to find its natural or neutral position by letting go of the muscles.

Be Patient

Always remember that as an adult, you have a lot of set ways of doing things. This includes your posture. You will need enough time and consistent effort to learn and be able to maintain these important alignments at the same time. More so while feeling relaxed. Because it'll take your mind and body enough time to adjust, you must be patient with yourself. One of the worst things you can do is rush yourself into mastering these alignments simultaneously. Remember, Rome wasn't built in a day, but they were busy laying bricks by the hour. So, be patient.

Qigong Stances

With Qigong, the five basic stances you need to learn include:

1. The Ma Bu, better known as the horse stance

2. The Gong Bu or the bow and arrow stance

3. The Xie Bu or the twisted stance

4. The Pu Bu or the sliding stance

5. The Xu Bu, better known as the empty stance

The Horse Stance

This is also called the *horse-riding stance*, and is one of the most popular basic stances in Qigong and Chinese martial arts in general. As you may glean from the name itself, this posture is akin to the one riding the back of a horse.

The more you research about this specific Qigong stance, you'll discover that they are a myriad number of variations of this. As such, I discourage obsessing about finding the one true or legitimate way of doing the horse stance. It's because certain variations are more appropriate than the others depending on the specific type of Qigong or Chinese martial arts you're performing. Still, all variations adhere to certain basic rules, and you must know why you're practicing Qigong, how you're doing it, and its basic theoretical foundations. The deeper your understanding of the horse stance, the better you'll be able to tweak it according to your goals, preferences, and needs.

What is the importance of the horse stance in Qigong? Normally, this is used in martial arts as an effective and efficient way of shifting from one technique or form to another. Practitioners use it specifically for developing stability, centering, and rooting or grounding. When it comes to Qigong, three of the most important foundations are stability, center, and roots. It can also be used for developing strength in the back, waist, and leg muscles.

Another important reason for using the horse stance when practicing Qigong is that it is a relaxed and comfortable posture that helps achieve a smooth flow of qi. As such, you'll need to learn how to assume this stance with minimal muscle support and using mostly your body's structure.

Later on, you will also use the three foundations of stability, center, and roots when assuming other narrower postures or stances. This will allow you to stand in a relaxed and strain-free manner for long periods, especially when doing stationary Qigong or standing meditations. In turn, you'll be able to feel comfortable and enable your qi to circulate freely.

When you learn to master the horse stance and practice regularly, you can also align your lower body much better. It's because the ma bu stance is the perfect stance for relaxing and aligning both your pelvis and legs. This realignment process needs time to complete, and initially, you will learn to relax your body from the outside in. As you do this, you'll first be able to release superficial tensions normally associated with larger muscle groups like the legs. Eventually, you learn to achieve relaxation in your deeper muscles and for the tendons, ligaments, fascia, etc.

If you look at this alignment process, it involves many baby steps or smaller alignments inside your body. When your body is relaxed, the many small corrections can appear to happen spontaneously because these small alignment processes naturally occur in your body when it's not strained or under tension. In this stance, you'll be able to slowly learn how to get in touch with your body tissues and structures. More importantly, you'll develop the ability to sense how interconnected they all are.

The ma bu or horse stance has its own set of characteristics, but many of these are not as obvious as they seem. That is why, as a beginner, I highly recommend applying them one at a time instead of all at once. Learning the horse stance requires patient practice and the gradual deepening of knowledge.

Let's talk about your feet first. Begin by standing with both feet at approximately twice the shoulder-width apart. Also, they should be parallel to each other, with the second toe pointing forward. Always be mindful about your feet staying flat on the ground while practicing the stance.

While you're in a horse stance, your body weight must be evenly distributed on both feet. You must use your center of gravity (the area of your lower Dantian) as the transmission point for your weight, from which it will move down to your legs. The end destination is the yong quan points of your feet. This is crucial because by doing it this way, your lower back is relaxed. Assuming this stance with a tight or tense lower back area may cause tension in the said area.

Initially, it'll feel like you're leaning a bit forward. As you practice this, you'll be able to develop the appropriate feeling.

Now, let's turn to your knees. They must be bent up an angle such that they line up vertically with your toes. To do this, gently push your knees outward in a sideways direction to align them as much as possible with your feet. Remember that discomfort, strain, or pain indicate that you are not doing it properly.

When you try to transition to a much wider stance, achieving the same level of alignment can be a bit more challenging and may take a bit more time in practice. The important thing is you're able to do it properly, so take your time mastering the position. If you insist on adopting a lower or wider stance without mastering knee alignment, you increase your risk for any injuries over time.

Speaking of a wider stance, double shoulder width is common in most martial arts and even in martial Qigong, but popular doesn't necessarily mean you should do it. How do you know how wide your stance should be? By how you feel.

As soon as you feel discomfort, strain, or pain, regardless of how narrow or wide your stance is, that is your red flag that you should make the necessary adjustments to your stance's width. To determine the appropriate or best one for you, you'll need to try various widths. The one in which you feel most comfortable and relaxed and lets you clearly find your center of gravity is the appropriate choice.

More than just the width of your stance in the ma bu posture, you must also pay attention to its height. This should be based on the kind and style of martial arts you are doing. In general, the deeper the stance is, the stronger your legs can become. That is why very deep ones are often used to develop excellent leg strength.

Going very deep often compromises proper posture or form because of its difficulty level. That is why you must gradually work on deepening your stance rather than going for a very deep one right off the bat. As a beginner, the higher stance versions of the ma bu should be your starting point.

Particularly in the Qigong practice, the height of your stance depends primarily on how you feel. If it is too low or deep, you will cause your leg muscles to tighten up and hinder the flow of your qi to your feet. If you're standing too high as a beginner, you won't be as stable as you haven't developed the necessary roots just yet.

While a higher stance is appropriate for beginners, you shouldn't assume a very high one either. Just high enough to make you feel comfortable without compromising your stability too much. To determine the idea stands hype, you can go lower, but only until the point, you are still comfortable in the legs. By doing this, you'll enjoy optimal stability, and by gradually deepening your stance over time, you can develop stronger leg muscles.

If you eventually want to achieve maximum qi flow through the legs, you must learn higher stances so your leg muscles are as relaxed as possible. As with deep stances, you can achieve stability even at very high stances by developing your roots over time. This is what many of the most experienced practitioners do.

Horse Stance Leg & Pelvic Arch

You can compare your pelvis and legs' structural connections to each other to the arch of stone bridges. If you are not familiar with how they look like, google them now for reference.

Stone bridges are made with such arches to ensure their ability to bear under huge weights that cross it regularly. The prominent stone in the middle of the bridge is called the keystone, and with your lower body, it's the pelvis. Just as stone bridges would collapse without a keystone, your body's structural integrity would be compromised without a healthy functioning pelvis. It bears the weight of the body and your head.

To transfer your upper body's weight down to your legs, you must learn to release the weight from your pelvis. When you're able to do this, you can successfully transition your upper body weight all the way to the ground.

It's easy to know when your lower body isn't aligned properly. You'll feel most of your torso's weight in your lower body, such as your calves, thighs, knees, and hips. You will also notice that your leg and hip muscles are tight because they're trying to maintain the balance of your weight. As mentioned earlier, if your leg muscles are tense, this will also constrict your qi's downward flow to your feet. Aside from that, it can also disrupt the flow of chief from the earth towards her upper body. In short, tense hip and leg muscles can constrict the efficient flow of qi in your body. That is why in

Qigong, the emphasis is on keeping your body relaxed during the practice.

You also have to be mindful of going too deep or too low, as with the Shaolin's Horse stance. Why? You risk structural misalignment as your upper body weight tends to push down between your legs. While you may strengthen your legs using very deep stances, the potential tradeoff is the inability to achieve optimal relaxation and, consequently, disrupted qi flow.

All this being said, you'll have an easier time learning how to assume the right pelvic posture by assuming a stance slightly wider than shoulder-width. As you progress in your Qigong beginners' journey, you can adopt a narrower stance, e.g., shoulder width, while still applying the same "arch" rule for the pelvis and the legs.

Your Head, Torso, and Spine

Ideally, your torso must be relaxed, centered, and upright. It's best to have your pelvis relaxed and hanging from your spine's base downwards when assuming the ma bu or horse stance. Your sacrum must neither be tilted forward nor backward, and you can achieve the ideal position by bending your knees and sinking from your kua (your body's energy gates). If you do this, you can achieve a relaxed lower back essential for optimal flowing qi.

The easiest way to achieve torso uprightness, centeredness, and relaxation is by imagining a piece of rope tied to the top of your head, and the other end is being pulled gently upward. This has the effect of gently pulling up your spine to lengthen and open it softly. Always be cognizant that your head must be vertically aligned to the center of your pelvis.

Also, slightly move your chin backward so you can straighten your neck. To do this, imagine pushing the area above your lips backward and, in the process, straightening your neck.

You need to keep your shoulder joints and chest open and relaxed. You may also rest the palms of your hands on your lower Dantian area. Finally, keep the tip of your tongue in contact with the roof of your mouth.

Getting Into the Horse Stance

To learn how to use your mind to lead the flow of your qi down into the earth and build strong energy routes to achieve stability, the ma bu or horse stance is your best bet. Here's how to do it:

1. Stand up with your feet double shoulder with apart. If it makes you feel uncomfortable or strained, you may use a narrower one instead.

2. Ensure both feet are parallel to each other, with the second toe pointing straight ahead.

3. Allow your body weight to descend from your center of gravity through your legs and, ultimately, to the yong quan points of your feet.

4. Keep your knees slightly bent up to where it is vertically aligned with your toes. Do not allow them to go forward beyond the toes.

5. Let your legs and pelvis form an arch as if you are riding on the back of a horse.

6. Relax your lower back and pelvis, with the latter hanging down from the bottom of your spine. Make sure your sacrum is centered, neither tilted forward nor pushed backward.

7. Then imagine somebody pulling a rope upward with the other end tide to the top of your head to gently pull up, lengthen, and open up your spine.

8. Straighten your neck by pushing your chin backward.

9. Relax and open your shoulder joints and chest. Put the palm of your hands on your lower dan tian.

10. Touch the roof of your mouth with the tip of your tongue.

11. Take slow, deep belly breaths and calm your mind.

At first, practice this stands for just a few minutes. You don't want to overwhelm yourself to where you could either get injured, burn out, or both. Just remember that the goal is to stand in a relaxed manner using this stance for at least 20 minutes, and you can accomplish this over time by gradually building up the skill and stamina. The proper form must always take precedence over the duration. Let your feeling of being comfortable and relaxed be your barometer. Just practice consistently every day, even for short periods.

The Bow Stance

After the horse stance, the next one you must learn is the bow stance. This is often used when shifting body weight from one leg to another and when changing our body's direction. As with the horse stance, you can perform this high or low according to how comfortable you feel.

Here are the steps on how to take this stance:

1. One foot is in front of the other

2. The foot in front should face directly forward

3. The front foot's knee must be on top of the foot and should not go beyond the vertical line extending from the toes. This ensures no excess strain is placed on the knee

4. Your hindfoot should face outward to the side at a 45-degree angle

5. Your pelvis must be facing forward

6. Drawback your fists so they'll be in line with your body

The Iron Cross Stance

If your shoulders are tight and if you tend to either slouch or hunch, this is the ideal stance to help you address or correct this posture. Here's how to get into the stance:

1. Stand with your feet parallel to each other and up to shoulder width

2. Relax your legs

3. Tuck your pelvis in as if you are seated on a stool. Doing this helps you to move your body from the waist freely and depressurizes your lower back nerves

4. Hold your head high and tuck your chin slightly in. Just imagine it being suspended from the center of the head by a string

5. Extend your arms to the side of your body at approximately shoulder height and reach outward. You should resemble a big cross with this stance

Consistency is Key

Fortunately, you need not spend months just to learn how to get into these stances properly. Just need to put in consistent time, attention, and effort in two learning how to perform them comfortably. Even as few as five minutes weekly in each stance can help you develop an awareness of which parts of your body are tense faster than you can imagine. Every breath you take suddenly expands and stretches your body, and with every exhale, you help it relax.

Consistently practicing these will allow you to significantly improve your posture over time and make it more comfortable and easier to hold these stances for longer periods. Eventually, you'll be able to open up your joints and feel more energy flowing in your body as you learn how to relax more and more while in these stances. You can develop the best energy flow through structurally sound and balanced postures by regularly practicing these static exercises.

Chapter 5: Qigong Breathing and Meditation

Two of the most important components of Qigong are the breath and the practice of meditation. In this chapter, we will talk about these two in detail.

Qigong Breathing Exercise Benefits

Qigong philosophy believes that a light heart and a healthy body can be achieved by going back or reclaiming our child-like nature. Instead of becoming more rigid, set in our ways, and stubborn as we grow old, Qigong allows us to achieve greater spontaneity, suppleness, and ability to be receptive as we age. You may picture each child's mind as a clear lake that reflects the sky above. You may achieve the same mental clarity by admitting or accepting that you don't know everything. What you do know may not always be right. Hence the saying "an intelligent person learns something new every day, and a wise person forgets something daily."

Young people live life as if they have limitless energy, but those reserves tend to decrease significantly as they age. The same happens to you, too. To replenish your personal batteries with vitality and regain a clear and open mind, you must practice what is called in Qigong as *the original breath.*

This kind of breathing is performed by breathing deeply like an infant using the lower abdomen. By doing this, you'll be able to redirect your focus away from your head down to your body. As you do this, you'll also be able to pull essential energy from out of the air surrounding you, which can help sustain and nourish your organs.

Qigong, particularly through breathing exercises, can help you focus on specific parts of your body, helping you restore its balance. By doing this, you'll be able to experience significant benefits, both physically and mentally.

One benefit is clearing your bladder meridian. Together with your kidneys, it helps flush out toxins from your body. This alone can be considered a very crucial process for your health and wellbeing.

But not only that, but your bladder's meridian also contributes greatly to your emotional balance. In particular, your bladder meridian emotions can help significantly improve your enthusiasm, self-confidence, and self-expression. It also helps foster intimacy, sexuality, control, and courage.

Considering how important these emotions are, can you imagine the serious emotional repercussions of an imbalanced bladder meridian? Some of these include the inability to make important decisions, jealousy, or anxiety.

This is just one example of an area that Qigong breathing can be most beneficial. It can also help you optimize other internal organs' function, including your spleen meridian and other qi points of your body.

Qigong breathing can help you harmonize your entire body by promoting qi's best flow throughout your body. It can also help you enjoy regular personal quiet time, fostering greater mindfulness and a clear mind. That is why when it comes to Qigong breathing, there's practically no downside.

Qigong Breathing Techniques

The Original Breath

As the name implies, this is the most basic breathing technique you can practice in Qigong. Here's how to do it properly:

1. You can do this by sitting down on a chair or cushion or by standing up. The key is to find the right balance for your spine, i.e., long and stretched yet relaxed. This is important because the flow of your qi is maximized with good posture alignment. On the other hand, access muscular tension associated with perfectionism can significantly constrict your qi's flow.

2. If you choose to perform this while standing up, make sure both your feet are parallel, about shoulder-width apart, and your knees are soft and slightly bent.

3. Next, fold your hands on top of your navel and observe your breathing.

4. Gradually, take longer, deeper, and smoother breaths.

5. Breathe using your lower abdomen. You'll be able to do this through your hands that are folded on top of your navel. When you are doing this correctly, you'll know when you see your belly expanding as you breathe in and drawing back inwards as you exhale.

6. If this is your first time doing breathwork, don't be discouraged if you're not able to get this right the first time. The important thing is to practice this consistently, and over time, you'll be able to learn how to breathe like a baby, i.e., barely breathe properly and do it naturally.

Another way you can tell you have learned to do this properly and naturally if it feels like your lungs are gently massaging your belly organs. Also, rejuvenation, feeling centered, and being relaxed are other ways to confirm that you're doing it right. Don't overstrain, and when you feel it's becoming uncomfortable, you may need to adjust accordingly.

Kidney Breathing

In the medical application of Qigong, physiology and energy are determined by specific internal organs. The lungs are primarily responsible for getting energy from the air. But the kidneys are primarily responsible for pulling the air energy in your lungs to bring it even deeper to the rest of your body. You may think of your kidneys as rechargeable batteries, which is where you can store air energy for future use, but just like physical batteries, they also get depleted over time. Through kidney breathing, you'll be able to recharge those batteries, massage your kidneys, and make your diaphragm stronger at the same time. If you forgot, the kidneys are positioned in your lower back area, with each kidney on one side of your spine. On top of them, you'll find your adrenal glands.

Kidney breathing is done best while standing up, ideally after performing the original breath exercise. Here's how to do it:

1. Stand with both feet parallel to each other and about shoulder-width apart. Just like the original breath, you must also keep your knees slightly bent and soft. Make sure that your knees never go ahead of your toes.

2. Now, place your hands on your lower back with your palms holding your lower back just above your hips and the fingers pointing downward toward your spine and sacrum.

3. Next, tuck your tailbone beneath your torso. An easy way to do this is by imitating a monkey trying to move its tail forward between its legs. By doing this, you'll be able to naturally straighten out your lower spine's natural curve.

4. Similar to how you expand your belly in the original breath, use your hands to feel your lower back expand. Unlike the movement in your belly, it'll be more subtle.

5. As you breathe out, use your hands to feel your lower back to contract or relax.

6. As you breathe in this position, start to slightly tilt your hips with every breath. While breathing in, tuck your tailbone beneath your body to curve your lower back slightly like how a monkey moves its tail forward beneath its legs.

7. As you exhale, resume your lower spine's natural curve by untucking your tailbone or bringing the monkey tail back. As you do this, be careful to do this slowly, softly, and smoothly to minimize your risks for spinal disc injuries, especially if you have a history of it.

8. To enhance your lower back's movement, you can slightly constrict or tense your abdominal muscles. By doing this, you won't be able to expand your belly as you breathe, but instead, it will be redirected to your lower back or the kidney area.

9. As your diaphragm and lungs are pushed downward and back, your adrenal glands and kidneys can enjoy a good massage and, in the process, improve both blood cleansing and hormonal activities.

Kidney breathing can be a bit challenging to perform, especially initially. However, it will help you strengthen your diaphragm in the long run. Ultimately, this can help you make breathing more natural and much easier. If you have lower back pain, this exercise can be therapeutic and provide adequate support for your lumbar spine.

Cleansing Breath

The third Qigong breathing exercise is, as the name implies, one that helps you energize and clean your body. In the process, it will also help you achieve a calm mind. If you've ever felt stressed, tired, or lethargic in the middle of the afternoon, the cleansing breath exercise can help you feel rejuvenated and relaxed. It is not only easy to learn, but it only takes up to 10 minutes every day to practice or as short as needed to give you an energy boost in the afternoon. Here's how to do it:

1. Look for a quiet place where you can practice the cleansing breath in a relaxed manner without being disturbed. Ideally, do it sitting on a chair that allows you to have good posture with your neck and back straight and with both your feet flat on the floor. During the exercise, don't cross your legs or feet.

2. Next, put your hands on top of your lap in a folded position with the right one on top of the left. If you prefer, you may place them on your knees separately instead.

3. Let the tip of your tongue touch your palate, i.e., the roof of your mouth just at the back of your upper teeth. Keep it there for the rest of the exercise.

4. Take deep breaths and relax your body before proceeding with the exercise.

5. Just like with the original breath, this exercise involves deep belly breathing, where you expand your belly instead of your chest when you inhale and let your belly draw back in as you breathe out. With each belly breath, you're able to fill your lungs with air up to its full capacity. Every time you exhale, ensure that you get as much air out of your lungs as possible.

6. Start the exercise by breathing slowly through your mouth. During the exhale, picture in your mind's eye dark-colored toxins and carbon dioxide departing from every part of your body.

7. On the next breath, do it slowly through your nose and visualize healing white energy and oxygen being distributed to and absorbed by all parts of your body. As it does so, your entire body is cleansed and nourished.

8. Hold the breath and as you do, continue visualizing the white energy and oxygen nourishing and cleansing your entire body. Then, exhale as much air from your lungs, also visualizing dark-colored toxins and carbon dioxide exiting your body.

9. Repeat the entire process for about 5 to 10 minutes every day.

How long should you hold your breath, and how many seconds should each inhale and exhale require? The ideal counts are 2-1-4, i.e., exhale in multiple counts of two seconds, inhale in multiple counts of 1 second, and hold your breath for multiple counts of four seconds. If it's too much to process initially, start using the box breathing technique. This means inhaling, holding the breath exactly, and holding the exhale position for the same length of time, e.g., 5-5-5-5 or 4-4-4-4. Again, the key here is that you shouldn't feel strained with the duration. Increase it over time, without too much strain.

Breathing this way can help improve blood and oxygen circulation to your brain and other body parts of your body. It will also help promote relaxation and optimal flow of qi in your meridians and organs. Over time, practicing the cleansing breath regularly can help you achieve a calmer mind and greatly reduce your life stress.

Reverse Breathing, Daoist Style

Compared to the first three, this one can be a bit more challenging to perform. Its primary goal is to intensify the meridian flow and purify the body. As such, it is a very good breathing exercise when performing Qigong movements or meditating.

The best way to master this breathing style is by learning how to breathe properly first. In particular, you must learn yogic breathing first. When you're able to do that, you can start on the Daoist reverse breathing technique. Here's how to perform this technique:

1. Sit down with your shoulders, neck, and head relaxed.

2. Touch your palate or the roof of your mouth using the tip of your tongue.

3. Keep your spine straight and long.

4. Put both hands on your lower abdomen with the right hand on top of the left one.

5. Breathe in through your chest, letting your ribs expand. When this happens, let your lower abdomen contract.

6. Allow your lower abdomen, just below your navel, to pull closer to your spine. When this happens, you should be able to feel it move away from your hands in a gentle and scooping manner. This helps your qi flow up your spine.

7. When you breathe out, allow your belly to resume its original position.

8. Perform this breathing movement ten times.

While this type of breathing can be more challenging to learn than the first three, it will be a great breathing technique for meditating or doing Qigong. Don't be impatient. Take your time learning this breathing technique because it'll be worth doing right.

When you combine this with a movement-based practice like Qigong, it's important to coordinate both. Ideally, do this by exhaling as you move your body and inhaling while holding a position.

Box-Breathing

Of all the breathing techniques thought in this chapter, this is probably the simplest and easiest to perform. This technique was popularized by former US Navy Seal and best-selling author Mark Divine in his popular book "Unbeatable Mind." It's called box breathing because all four phases of this exercise, i.e., the inhale, holding the inhale, exhale, and holding the exhale, all require the same length of time. Breathe through the nose only.

Divine recommends five seconds for each phase, but if it's too long for you, you can start with something shorter and gradually lengthened the periods. Initially, go for at least five minutes per session. Gradually increase the duration over time.

This is also a very practical way to relax and calm yourself down when you're feeling highly stressed or anxious. After a few breathing cycles, you'll notice your heart rate slowing down to help you relax.

Prepare for the Breathing Exercises

To get the most out of your Qigong breathing sessions, there are things you can do beforehand. Some include:

1. Putting yourself in the right mental state, i.e., one that's relaxed and not in a hurry.

2. Settling yourself in a place that is quiet and distraction-free.

3. Block off time from your schedule to ensure the consistent practice of these techniques. Consistency is key for experiencing the benefits of these breathing exercises.

4. Wear comfortable fitting clothes to ensure free-flowing qi. Tight clothes hinder deep breathing and can constrict the flow of your qi.

Chapter 6: The Dantian: Activating Core Energy

What is the Dantian? In traditional Chinese medicine, this is frequently called the stored *energy center* for the body. It's also worth noting that a Dantian isn't the same as a chakra. The latter is an energy gateway, while the Dantian is an energy storage center.

The Three Dantians

Each of the three is closely linked to specific elements: fire, water, and earth. These are the lower, middle, and upper Dantians.

The Lower Dantian

You can find this in your lower abdomen area, about three fingers below your navel and two fingers behind it. This Dantian is responsible for creating your essence or jing energy. Traditional Chinese medicine considers the lowered Dantian as the "superior ultimate" of all the Qigong treasures.

It is also called the golden stove. In ancient Chinese culture, the lower Dantian is believed to be the foundation for several important aspects of martial arts and Qigong-like balancing, breathing, rooted standing, and awareness of one's entire body. Many also call it the roots of the tree of life and where a person's internal energy or qi comes from, common in the Chinese, Japanese, and Korean cultures.

Many of those who teach Buddhism and Taoism instruct their followers to prioritize their Dantian because it allows them to learn of the universe's greater mind. Ultimately, it helps activate their higher state of consciousness or samadhi.

One reason this Dantian is believed to be the most important of the three treasures it's because of its position. Unless it's activated and opened, you won't be able to sense or feel you're two other Dantians, i.e., the upper and middle ones. When it's blocked or closed, which is the case for most people, you won't be able to tap into your renewable energy. Instead, you must get energy mainly from sources that are not renewable both inside your body and in your environment. This tends to deplete not just your internal resources but your environmental ones as well.

But if you're able to activate and keep this gateway open, you'll be evil to enjoy abundant energy directly from its source. This energy type can also flow freely through your chakras and meridians, so every muscle, organ, and body part is energized. Along the way, thoroughly energizing every part of your body can help you relax and feel more confident, too.

This type of energy also helps clear your channels of the negative energies absorbed by your body's cells throughout the years. Some also call this the *cellular purification process.*

When you have successfully activated your lower Dantian, this cleansing energy you can freely travel from your body's center up through your chakra system. Along the way, it clears your energy pathways such that qi can freely flow and nourish every cell in your body. Ultimately, it keeps pushing upward until it arrives at the top of your head, where it generates highly positive emotions and illuminates your entire body, mind, and spirit.

As you do this, you'll be able to reconnect to a state of love and openness often called enlightenment or samadhi. This includes a process of being born, receiving global and ancestral karma, experiencing sufferings, dying a thousand deaths, the ability to establish a divine connection, divine transformation, and to experience the entire human transformation journey.

You may also think of these as the source and rise of kundalini energy. Particularly in Hindu culture, kundalini is believed to be strong divine energy that resembles a coiled snake at the root chakra or base of a person's spine. Viewed as a divine feminine power or shakti energy, kundalini energy is created primarily through methods like pranayama breathing, meditation, mantra chanting, tantra, and asana practice.

Many practitioners look at the Taoist and Hindu energy concepts as being slightly different in terms of what they do but basically have the same source. You may think of your lower Dantian as the creator or manufacturer of your vital life energy and the kundalini you awaken as the fuel that powers the creator or generator.

Middle Dantian

This one is positioned at your heart level, and it's the center of power for your emotions and thoughts. The middle Dantian is linked to your internal organs' health (particularly your thymus gland) and the respiratory system. Called the crimson palace, your middle Dantian produces vital energy or qi, which is your air energy or, in a figurative sense, your life force.

The heart is the power center of love, from which all things are created. It's the only healing force in the world, and as such, it's important for achieving optimal health and well-being.

Many people feel unloved simply because their middle Dantian has yet to open fully. If you don't feel as loved despite knowing in your mind that people do love you, your middle Dantian probably isn't fully opened yet. As you learn to activate and open this one up, you'll be able to feel an increasing amount of love in your life.

If that were the case, you might be wondering why you are unconsciously keeping your lower Dantian from fully opening up? Because the lower Dantian tends to push powerful energy up to your heart that manifests itself as love. When this happens, you may awaken your kundalini energy, which can lead to a surge of emotions, leading to the cleansing of emotional pain. Because this can feel unpleasant or painful, the natural tendency is to avoid it altogether, and thus, it's probably the reason you and many other people keep your lowered Dantian from fully opening up. However, the pain or discomfort is necessary to allow the kundalini or qi energy to cleanse and clear your meridian paths and facilitate optimal flow to the upper Dantian and crown chakra, also known as *Sahasrara.*

Your lower Dantian has the power to amplify the love you receive and give to others. When you can properly develop or activate your middle Dantian, you can ensure that the positive force coming from the lower one can reach the upper one. When this happens, the potential for optimal health and well-being is maximized.

Upper Dantian

The last of the three Dantians is positioned between and above your eyebrows. This is commonly referred to in Hindu culture as the *ajna chakra* or the third eye. The organ that is most associated with this specific power center is the pineal gland. The spirit or consciousness is the primary area of concern of the upper Dantian.

Others also called this Dantian a muddy pellet and believe this power center is the one that creates the shen energy in Chinese culture. Here, once spirit or shen is further refined into pure consciousness.

When your vital life forces can reach this power center, your brain can experience a huge burst of energy that can permeate every energetic and biological system in your body. As this happens, a powerful light floods these systems, silencing your ego or conscious mind. In turn, more divine intelligence is available for your brain to perform a vast number of complex functions. It allows you to achieve optimal cognitive performance and the sense of being one with the universe.

Synthetically, this same level of consciousness can also be awakened through psychoactive drugs like MDMA, certain types of mushrooms, DMT, and other psychoactive plants like ayahuasca. However, these are unnatural ways of doing so, and because they can rapidly bring people to such a level of consciousness, they may not be ready for the experience.

But with Qigong, you can gradually achieve such a level of consciousness at a pace comfortable for you. As such, your experience will be more beneficial than traumatic or super intense.

Dantian Weaknesses

Your Dantians are crucial for optimal health and well-being within your practice of Qigong. That is why you must also be familiar with signs that tell you when getting weak.

For example, your vital energy can float upward when it's not focused on your lower Dantian. When this happens, you risk disturbing your upper Dantian. This may negatively affect you emotionally and mentally, making minor nuisances and issues feel worse and bigger than they really are.

If left unchecked, it may cause you to lose sight of your life's essence and purpose, leading to an unfulfilled life. Unresolved, these may eventually lead to disease and distress.

When your lower Dantian performs poorly, you must get more energy from your prenatal qi reserves every day. Considering this is a finite resource, you won't be able to sustain this practice in the long run. When your lower Dantian is functioning optimally, it's like you're running on solar, wind, or nuclear energy - all of which are renewable. Otherwise, it's like trying to run on fossil fuel or coal that is limited in quantities.

When your middle Dantian is closed, it will be challenging for you to connect with your emotions or your heart. As a result, it will feel like you're not receiving enough love in your life despite the contrary. It will also affect your ability to love other people, and you'll likely feel uninspired, unmotivated, and disconnected from others.

Finally, it is very hard to look forward to the future when your upper Dantian is not performing well. Some ways you can tell this is happening are when you feel lacking in vitality or when people tell you you've lost the sparkle in your eyes.

This isn't something to be taken lightly because often, the way we live our lives is primarily influenced by this area. We risk living a life devoid of purpose and fulfillment ask there will be a disconnection from the two other Dantians, i.e., the heart and the essence. The best way to live life is through synergistic cooperation between the lower, middle, and upper Dantians.

Strengthening Your Dantian

So, what can you do to strengthen your Dantian when it's weak?

Given that it's the most important of the three treasures, it is important to ground and strengthen your lower Dantian first. If you do this, the two other Dantians will also benefit from it. This doesn't mean working on your lower Dantian is all that's needed to strengthen the whole. You'll still need to strengthen the two other

Dantians, but if you focus on the lower part first, it can be much easier to improve the others.

How do you strengthen your lower Dantian? While acupuncture treatment is the best way to do it, practicing lower Dantian breathing allows the treatment to optimize the Dantian strengthening results.

Lower Dantian strengthening exercises allow you to better hold and build your qi. It also gives you a stronger core, which improves your body's stability and lowers your risk of falling off balance and getting injured. Through lower Dantian breathing, you can be happier, less stressed, and healthier.

Here's a simple meditative lower Dantian breathing exercise you can do regularly for strengthening said area:

1. Assume and hold an erect posture.

2. Keep your feet parallel to each other and about shoulder-width apart.

3. Keep your knees slightly bent and soft, so the joints don't bear the entire weight.

4. Pull your pelvis forward while keeping your spine straight.

5. Keep your head straight with your neck pulled back.

6. Think of a string passing through your head down to your spine all the way to the ground between your feet.

7. Take a deep breath and bring it down all the way to your lower Dantian through the imaginary string.

8. When you inhale, expand your lower abdomen as your diaphragm expands, too.

9. Then, visualize a warm ball of energy in your lower Dantian area, which is about five fingers below your navel and three fingers behind it.

10. Every time you inhale, imagine the energy ball growing.

11. As you exhale, see the same ball shrinking.

12. Do this a couple of times, and afterward, put your palms on top of your lower Dantian and continue the breathing exercise. Doing so can help you become conscious of your Dantian during the exercise.

13. If you're a man, your right hand should be on top of the left one. If you're a woman, the left should be on top of the right.

14. Practice this exercise for 10 to 15 minutes every day and gradually increase the duration over time at a comfortable pace.

You may also strengthen your lower Dantian through mindful movements such as aikido or tai chi. In these martial arts, the primary focus is on your lower Dantian. By focusing on this, you become more grounded and stable physically.

After strengthening your lower Dantian, it's time to focus on the upper one. Here's a practical exercise to help you do that.

1. Start by focusing your attention on the crown of your head. Imagine an 8-shaped figure on top of it lying horizontally across your scalp. Choose any point on the surface of the imaginary 8-shaped figure. Imagine there's a pen fixed on that position. Slowly "draw" an 8-shaped figure on your crown by moving your head instead of the "pencil."

2. Coordinate this movement with your breathing to activate your cranial pump. To do this, imagine your cranial plates being pulled apart to widen their seams as you exhale. As you inhale, imagine the opposite act, i.e., your cranial blades being pulled together with its seams narrowing.

3. Repeat steps one and two at least eight times.

4. Next, visualize the eight-shaped figure going down into your brain and, as it does, see it transform into a Mobius strip, which is an 8-shaped figure with no intersecting points.

5. Imagine a thread by visually tracing a line that runs across your brain that ghost near the corpus callosum, which resides between your brain's two hemispheres.

6. When you practice this exercise regularly, you'll be able to achieve greater harmony between your right and left brain. This can help you combine your creative and analytical thinking skills, which are your right and left brain's key functions, respectively.

7. At certain times, slow things down and create a long "nnnnnnnn" sound with your tongue touching your pallet and your mouth half-closed. You can direct the sound waves produced towards your cranial vault. In turn, this can conduct the vibratory response in the middle of your brain, where traditional bridges and gateways to the spiritual plane are located, such as the pineal and pituitary glands, the thalamus, and the hypothalamus.

8. When you're done, express gratitude and smile your left and right brain.

Strengthening your Dantian can take time. Hence, be patient and continue regularly practicing at a pace comfortable for you. It will come, I assure you.

Chapter 7: Practical Qigong: Warm-Ups

Before practicing Qigong movements, remember this - despite how gentle and flowing the movements are, you should still warm up before proceeding. Here are some excellent warm-up movements to prepare for your Qigong sessions.

1. Finger stretches: start by putting the palm of your hand down on a flat surface or a table. Gently, make your fingers as straight as possible against it without forcing or putting a strain on your joints. Hold it's for 30 to 60 seconds before releasing and repeat at least four times.

2. Wrist rotations: clasp both hands and perform several rotations, starting with a clockwise movement followed by a counterclockwise one.

3. Elbow rotations: bring your arms up to your sides to form a big cross with your body. While keeping your upper arms (biceps and triceps) steady, move your forearms in a circular motion several times. Start with a forward motion followed by a backward motion.

4. Shoulder rotations: rotate each of your upper arms at shoulder level several times, starting with the forward movement followed by a backward one. To have an idea of how to do this properly, imagine drawing large circles on each side of your body using your elbows.

5. Waist rotations: move your hips sideward, forward, to the other side, and backward in a smooth and circular flow. Perform several repetitions for each direction.

6. Knee rotations: stand with both feet close together and slightly bent and both hands resting on top of your knees. In a smooth circular motion, move your knees to one side, forward, through the other side, to the back, and back to the side for several repetitions. Then, do them again for the same number of reps flowing in the opposite direction this time.

7. Ankle rotations: start by planting the toes of one of your feet on the ground and use it as the base on which you'll rotate your ankle for several repetitions in one direction before reversing the movement for the same number of reps. Do the same for the other foot.

8. Spine rotations: stand with your feet parallel to each other and about shoulder width, with one arm raised forward and the other up your back. Look at your backhand by turning your head, then swing your arms down by your sights and up again to switch hand positions. Imagine doing a running man position with your arm switching positions while running. When forward raised arm goes to the back, turn your head so you can look at it. This creates a gentle twist in your spine. Repeat this movement several times smoothly and rhythmically.

Chapter 8: Practical Qigong: Essential Exercises

Each exercise is closely related to a specific organ in your body, each having its specific peak activity periods within the day/night. These are arranged in chronological order based on their related organ's peak activity, starting with the gall bladder that peaks between 11:00 pm and 1:00 am.

To get the most out of your daily Qigong routine, start it by performing the exercise whose related organ's peak activity coincides with the time of your practice. For example, start with the Body Bend & Head Swing exercise if you plan to do Qigong between 5:00 am and 7:00 am. Then, just follow the sequence of the exercises below to end with the exercise before the one you started with. In this example, you'll end the session with the Path-Clearing Dragon. Adjust accordingly based on the time you'll work out.

Again, prioritize proper form. You need not perform all the exercises at once. Learn one or two, and once you've mastered them, add another one until you've mastered all the 12 exercises.

The Tiger's Back Stretch

This exercise is closely related to your gallbladder, and its peak activity is between 11:00 pm to 1:00 am. Here's how to perform the exercise:

1. Start by assuming the bow stance. Your hands should be in front of you, with the right one held high in the left one held low.

2. Turn your body to the left and as you do so, breathe in.

3. Lower your stance and extend both arms forward while exhaling.

4. Bring your hands up above your head as you continue to exhale. Let your gaze follow your hands.

5. Finish the move by looking behind you.

6. Return to your original position by turning right and as you do, inhale.

7. Repeat the movement by turning in the opposite direction, i.e., turning your body to the right with your left hand held high and your right one held low.

The Four Body Movements

This exercise is related to your liver, whose peak activity is from 1:00 am to 3:00 am. Here are the steps:

1. Begin by assuming the bow stance.

2. Turn to your left side and assume a lunging position. Exhale as you do this.

3. As you perform a lunge, make sure that your knees never go beyond your toes to prevent knee strain.

4. Lunge backward (to the right while still facing left) to shift your weight to your right leg. Inhale as you do this and make sure your knee never goes beyond the toes.

5. While maintaining this position, bend at the waist to lean your upper body towards your left leg. Keep your lower back as straight as possible to minimize risks for strain and injuries. Make sure your pelvis is over your right leg throughout the movement, too.

6. Go back to the forward lunging position to shift your body weight to your left leg again. Exhale as you do this and make sure the left knee never goes beyond the toes.

7. Continue exhaling as you turn to the right to return to the original or starting bow stance. Repeat this in the opposite direction.

The Path-Clearing Dragon

This exercise is related to your lungs, whose speak activity is between 3:00 a.m. and 5:00 a.m. Here are the steps to performing it:

1. Begin by standing in a horse stance.

2. Clench your fists and draw back your elbows so they are directly in line with your waist.

3. Turn to your left side, ending in a bow stance.

4. Exhale as you bring out your left fist in front of you from your center, as if you're punching somebody but in a very slow manner. Stop short of locking your elbows.

5. Bring up your extended left arm in a circular manner to bring your fist behind you. Inhale as you do this and keep your gaze on your fist.

6. Reverse the motion to bring your fist back directly above your head and continue breathing in as you do this.

7. Bring your fist back in front of your body, with the arm remaining extended. Exhale as you do this.

8. Cap off the movement by bringing your fist back in line with your waist to resume the starting position. Inhale as you do this.

9. Repeat this sequence facing the other direction and using your right arm.

Body Bend & Head Swing

This exercise involves your large intestine, whose peak activity is between 5:00 am to 7:00 am. Follow these steps to perform it properly:

1. Start by assuming a low horse stance and rest both hands on top of your knees so you can use your arms to support your body weight and avoid straining your lower back throughout the movement.

2. Use your upper body to draw a circle. Do this by bringing down your body towards the left, to the center, then bring it back up to the right side before returning to your original horse stance position. Try to make the biggest circle you can with your head. Inhale throughout this movement.

3. Repeat this to complete one sequence, going the other direction and exhaling throughout the movement.

4. Repeat the sequence. This time, inhale while going to the right and exhale as you go left.

The One-Arm Raise

This exercise involves your stomach, which reaches peak activity between 7:00 am to 9:00 am. Here are the steps:

1. Start by standing with your feet close together.

2. In front of your naval, bring your palms together with the left one on top of your right.

3. Bring your left hand up and the right hand down simultaneously while tiptoeing, breathing out while doing these.

4. Make a large circle with your hands, ending with your right hand up high and your left hand down low. Breathe in as you do this.

5. As you resume a flat-footed position, bring your palms close together with the right hand over the left this time. Continue inhaling as you do this.

6. Repeat the movement, this time in the other direction. Put your right palm over your left palm, then circle your hands in the opposite direction. As you perform this movement, inhale, then exhale as you return to the starting position.

The Hind-Looking Crane

The exercise involves your spleen, with activity peaking between 9:00 is to 11:00 am. Perform this exercise through these steps:

1. Start by assuming the ma bu or horse stance. Raise both arms to the sides up to shoulder level, inhaling as you do this.

2. Lower your arms to your sides and face your left side. Bring your right arm up forward and your left one backward. As you do this, turn both feet such that each forms a 45-degree angle facing outward, i.e., the left foot forms a 45-degree angle to the left while the right one forms a 45-degree angle to the right. Continue inhaling as you do these.

3. Do the same movement but this time, turning towards your right side. Exhale as you do this to complete one sequence.

4. Repeat the whole sequence. This time, breathe in while turning to your right, then breathe out as you turn to your left.

The Wing-Beating Wild Goose

The organ related to this exercise is your heart, whose peak activity is between 11:00 am to 1:00 pm. Here's how correctly performed the exercise:

1. Start by assuming a horse stance.

2. Clench your fists and bring your elbows back such that your fists are in line with your body. Inhale as you do this.

3. Raise your fists upward over your head touch your nape, keeping your elbows bent. In the process, you are raising your elbows above and slightly in front of your head. Exhale as you do this.

4. Reverse the movement and bring your elbows back to their original position, then rolling them up and forward in a circular motion. The circular movement of your elbows by pointing them directly forward. Continue breathing out while doing this.

5. Straighten your arms to extend them forward. Extend your fingers as well while continuing to exhale.

6. Go back to your starting position by bringing back your fists beside your waist. Breathe in as you do.

Wind-Punching

This exercise is linked to your small intestine, whose peak activity is between 1:00 pm to 3:00 pm. Here are the steps to performing it:

1. Begin by assuming a horse stance with your elbows drawn back so your fists are in line with your waist. Breathe in ask you do the latter.

2. Extend your left arm and bring your left fist forward as if punching something in front of you slowly and steadily while breathing out. Don't lock your arms but instead, stop short of locking your elbows instead.

3. While keeping your upper arm and elbow fixed pointing forward, draw a circle with your left fist by swinging it down toward your center, then up and forward in front of you, with your left arm extended forward and back to the punch position. Continue exhaling.

4. Next, turn your hand over and stretch your fingers while continuing to breathe out.

5. To conclude the movement, return your left fist to its original position beside your waist. Inhale as you do this.

6. Perform the same movement with the other arm.

The Black Tiger Straight Waist

This exercise is closely linked to your bladder, and its activity peaks between 3:00 pm to 5:00 pm kick it. Here are the steps to perform this:

1. Stand straight with your feet about shoulder-width apart and arms to the sides. Keep your knees slightly bent.

2. Bend forward at the waist and interlock your fingers as you inhale. Keep your lower back straight throughout the movement to minimize risks for lower back strain or injuries.

3. Return to your standing position and raise your arms up and forward to shoulder level. Breathe out as you do this and keep your fingers locked.

4. Bring down your arms and pull them back as far as you can while breathing in.

5. Reverse the movement by swinging them forward, up, and backward past your head. At this point, you're back should be slightly arched backward. Exhale as you perform this movement.

6. Reverse the movement and bring down your arms while continuing to exhale.

7. Raise your arms forward, up, and back over your head again while continuing to exhale.

8. As you bring them down again, do your sides, breathe in.

The Horse-Riding Archer

In this exercise, you'll be working your kidneys, which reach their peak activity between 5:00 pm to 7:00 pm. Here are the steps:

1. Start by assuming the horse stance with your arms to the sides.

2. Turn your head to your left. Bring your arms up such that your left hand is in front of your left shoulder with its left finger stretched, and your right hand is just behind it with all fingers extended. Inhale while doing these.

3. Extend your left arm to your left side and think of your index finger as a bow by which you will launch arrows later. Bring back your right hand to the center of your chest or in front of your right nipple as if you were pulling back the bow's string to launch an arrow. As you do these, breathe out.

4. Bring your arms down back to your sides and inhale while doing so.

5. Perform the same movements, this time facing your right side and with opposite arms and hands.

Turn & Gaze

The second to the last exercise is closely linked to your pericardium or circulation sex organ. Its peak activity lies between 7:00 pm and 9:00 pm, and here's how to practice the exercise:

1. Begin by assuming a horse stance with arms to your sides.

2. Circle both hands such that the right hand is at the bottom of the circle while the left one is on top. As you form the circle, breathe in.

3. Bring your hands to close together and continue inhaling while doing so.

4. Press both hands forward with your right-hand low and the left-hand high. Exhale while doing this.

5. Twist your body to the left, keeping your eyes fixed on your left hand and continuing to exhale as you do.

6. Reverse the movement and twist to your right side, still fixing your eyes on the left hand while breathing out.

7. Return to the middle and face forwards while inhaling.

8. Create a circle using your hands again. This time bring your right hand to the top of the circle and your left hand to the bottom. Continue inhaling.

9. Bring your palms together in front of your body as you continue breathing in.

10. Repeat steps 1 to 9 but this time, exhaling while you bring your hands forward with your right hand above and your left hand below. Continue exhaling while twisting your body to the right and then to the left.

Hands Pushing the Sky

This exercise involves your triple warmer organ, the peak activity of which is from 9:00 pm to 11:00 pm. Here are the steps:

1. Stand up straight with your feet about shoulder-width apart and your hands to your sides.

2. Next, raise both arms to your sides until they are at shoulder height or parallel to the ground. Breathe in when you do this movement.

3. Bring your hands on top of your head and interlock your fingers while continuing to breathe in.

4. Turn your palms downside up.

5. While keeping your fingers interlocked, push your hands upward and extend your arms while exhaling. Simultaneously, raise your body up by tiptoeing and look upward.

6. Bring your hands back down to the top of your head, still breathing out.

7. Turn your palms upside down, with fingers still interlocked, so your palms are touching the top of your head.

8. Unlock your fingers, straighten your arms, and lower them down back to shoulder level or until parallel to the ground. Breathe in while doing this.

9. At this position, rotate your palms so they are now facing the floor.

Complete the sequence by bringing your arms down back to your sides, exhaling as you do so.

Chapter 9: The Qi Diet

There is a saying: we are what we eat. Our general health and wellbeing depend largely on the quality of our diet. We can optimize health and wellbeing with a healthy diet and vice versa.

Qigong is primarily known for its movements, postures, and breathing, but it's also influenced by nutrition. Remember that our qi or internal life force energy is also affected by what we put inside our bodies. These include the air we breathe and the food we eat.

At the most basic level, the human body gets its energy in the form of calories from the foods consumed. More than just delivering essential caloric energy, they also provide our body's cells with elemental energies, which can also affect our mind and spirit. Hence, what we eat is crucial for optimizing the benefits of Qigong.

Individualized

One of the more important characteristics of a Qigong-aligned diet is individualization. Simply put, this means an optimal diet is most likely different from one person to another, both in terms of quantity and quality of food.

Given this, how would you know the best foods for your health and wellbeing as part of the Qigong practice? Honestly, there is no one best answer to that question because there is really not one best diet that applies to everybody. You are a unique person as much as everybody else differs from one another, and what may constitute the best Qigong diet for you may differ from what constitutes the same for me and everybody else. To that extent, you must pay close attention to your body and how certain foods affect how you feel and how you perform.

Luckily, you need not labor over studying different types of food and their potential impact on your body because the human body itself is wise enough to know what foods are good and bad for it. Learn how to pay close attention to your body because it will help you discover which foods to focus on and what to avoid.

You also need to be honest with yourself about how specific types of food affect you after meals. Sometimes, we tend to justify our favorite food and drinks, even if they make us feel terrible after eating them. If you acknowledge their true effects on you, it'll be easier for you to eat optimally and experience Qigong's benefits.

There are certain foods whose post-meal effects are very glaring and obvious. Some of these post-eating impacts include nausea, pain in the tummy, or even fatigue. When the effects are very clear, there's no need for a careful evaluation.

But there are certain foods whose negative impacts aren't as obvious because they are so subtle. That is why unless you observe very obvious side effects, take the time to sit down with yourself and thoroughly check your energy levels and how you feel.

As you make this a habit, you'll develop the ability to easily notice have different types of food and drinks impact you afterward regardless of how subtle the effects may be. As Qigong is based on a subtle form of energy, the same goes for your diet.

When you're too busy with so many things or when you're running on autopilot, i.e., lack of mindfulness, it's very easy to ignore your qi. If you practice mindfulness in your life, you'll be able to slow things down enough to feel the changes in your qi and in other areas of your life, including nutrition, among others.

Food, the Elements, and Seasons

An important element or principle for eating for optimal health and wellbeing when it comes to Qigong is the relationship of food to specific elements and seasons.

With our dietary requirements, most of it is determined by our body's composition. Based on traditional Chinese medicine, a person comprises energy elements, or the five basic elements - earth, fire, wood, water, and metal.

While it's true that we all belong to the same ecosystem called nature, and our bodies are made of the same "materials," one way each of us differs from the other is the ratio and proportion or amount of each element. Just as modern science teaches that each person comprises a unique DNA code, traditional Chinese medicine uses the concept of the five elements to convey the same.

Based on this concept, you require specific types of foods and specific amounts, in ways different from everyone else's, based on the relative amounts and proportions of the five elements inside your body. Every type of food and taste has different effects on your elemental energies.

Take, for example, the fire element. It's probably obvious to you that this refers to the foods that are warm and spicy. How about the water element? It pertains to foods that are cooling and salty. Foods related to the wood element are warm and sour. Foods related to the metal element are generally pungent and mildly cooling. Foods related to the earth are neutral in temperature and tend to be sweet.

Here's a summary of each element's relationship to specific types of food and the particular organs involved:

1. Earth, yellowish and sweet foods, and the organs involved are the spleen and stomach.

2. Metal, white-colored spicy/acrid foods, and the organs involved are large intestines and lungs.

3. Water, blue/black-colored salty foods, and the organs involved are the bladder and kidneys.

4. Wood, green-colored sour foods, and the organs involved are the gallbladder and liver.

5. Fire, red-colored spicy or bitter food, and the organs involved are the small intestines and the heart.

After reading this, you'll be able to easily figure out how all these come together, especially if you're familiar with how the organs in your body work. Just like with other areas of Qigong, the relationship of the five elements with food and organs aren't arbitrary; but instead, they are based on sound principles and are linked to actual physical properties both of your body and your environment.

Foods that have yellowish color contain higher amounts of specific types of nutrients in as much as the other colored foods also contain higher amounts of specific types of nutrients.

More than just their colors, specific flavors also affect your body in different ways. For example, think about how your body reacts when you eat or bite a slice of lemon as compared to when you drink soda. The slice of lemon makes your mouth produce a lot of saliva, while the cold soda helps you feel refreshed and cool.

Such physical reactions aren't just limited to superficial ones. Similar reactions can happen with specific organs in the body responsible for digesting, absorbing, and using the nutrients.

How can you apply this information between the relationship of food, elemental energies, and organs to your Qigong diet? A few ways include:

1. Eat more sour food to activate your liver more.

2. Eat better foods to make your small intestines and heart more robust.

3. To achieve better activity balance among your organs, include a little of each type of flavor every time you eat.

4. To enjoy more nutrient-balanced meals, consider eating foods with a wide variety of colors per sitting.

More than just the elements, a diet optimized for Qigong's benefits consider the seasons. More than just affecting the environment you live in, seasons can also play a role in who you are as a person and your specific needs.

One very obvious example is alcohol. There's a reason why strong liquors tend to be very popular in countries with very cold weather: they help raise body temperature. Another example is cold lemonade. While very popular during the hot summer season, it's hardly in demand during the rainy and cold winter months.

Your body knows what it needs to achieve equilibrium during specific seasons. Hence, cravings for certain types of food and drinks according to the general climate and weather. During cold seasons, your body craves hot or heat-inducing food and drinks, while during hot and humid seasons, it craves for food and drinks that are cold.

Eating Habits

It's not just what you eat and drink that determines your health and wellbeing. How you eat has a big say, too. It's because food and drinks don't just contain nutrients but also, to some extent, emotions. That's why you're eating habits mustn't be just optimal for giving your physical body nourishment but emotional ones too.

You may be wondering, how do you "consume" or get enough nourishing emotions? One way is to take your time eating and not to hurry up your meals. While it's true that we live in a fast-paced society, it doesn't mean eating fast and mindlessly to rush to the next task is the best way to get needed calories. In fact, eating food in a very hurried manner and with little to no mindfulness increases the likelihood of you eating foods void of nourishing calories and eating more than what's needed.

But more than these, eating at a hurried and stressful pace can also make you feel more anxious and mentally and emotionally stressed. The point of eating is to replenish the body's nutrients and restore its vitality. Eating this way isn't just counterproductive - it's unhealthy, too. When you slow down your eating, you treat every meal as a sacred space to restore and rejuvenate your mind, body, and spirit.

What does eating mindfully actually mean? One of the most practical or objective ways of doing it is by chewing your food a minimum number of times with every bite. The ancient Taoist recommendation is at least 50 times. Considering this is too much for most people, you can go for 20 to 30 bites instead.

Why should you chew your food many times before swallowing every bite? It's because digestion doesn't start in the stomach - but *in the mouth*. Chewing food many times helps break it down substantially, and together with your saliva, it preps the food for optimal digestion and extraction of nutrients in the stomach once you swallow them. Therefore, taking your time to chew your food as long as possible can help your body get as many nutrients as it can from food. Doing so also helps you savor the taste for as long as possible, making mealtime even more joyful.

Another important eating habit to develop about a Qigong-friendly diet is never to drink cold beverages during meals. Why? Doing so increases the risk of quenching; they just in fires in your stomach. Instead, bear your meals with warm liquids to help optimize digestion in your stomach and allow your body to get the most nutrients out of every meal. It's best to drink cold or cool beverages outside of meals.

While this list isn't all-encompassing for mindful eating practices and optimal nourishment, it's a great place to start.

Yin, Yang, and Your Food

Food can also be characterized based on the principles of yin and yang. To be more specific, we were talking about the qualities of your food and drinks about can either, among other things:

1. Cool down or warm up your body

2. Dry your system or provide adequate moisture

3. Energize your internal organs or draw energy out of your body

With a little preparation and processing, the intrinsic qualities of food determine the impact on our bodies.

One of the basic qualities of food is that it provides warmth when cooked, just like raw food is more likely to help the body cool down. That is why, during cold seasons such as winter, cooked foods are more appropriate because they provide much-needed body warmth. But when you eat more raw foods during the summer, this can help alleviate the impact of a hot and humid environment on your body.

It seems that these characteristics are ingrained in the human psyche. Even without reading this, it's natural for people to prefer soups and stews and other cooked foods when it's cold, and during hot and humid seasons like summer, many people prefer raw fruits and salads. Regardless of how instinctive or basic this seems, you'll be able to tap into your natural intuition more deeply and more accurately apply these principles with more skill when you take the time to understand them in more detail.

Your Food and the Environment

As mentioned earlier, seasons or weather have a say on what types of food are best for us at any given time. Similar to this, our surrounding environment also matters. It's because weather or seasons are largely dependent on your location. Living in a tropical country like the Philippines, where it's hot and humid most of the year, eating body-cooling foods is appropriate. In very cold places like Antarctica, cooked foods are the way to go.

The relationship between food and the environment is also evident in the types of foods available in certain areas of the world. Tropical fruits, for example, are more abundant in countries that lie near the equator. It isn't a coincidence that such foods are best for mitigating the effects of hot weather in tropical countries. This is one way that nature brings balance to the environment and the people who live in it.

When you eat in harmony with the environment in which you live, it'll be easier for you to get all the necessary nutrients for optimal health and wellbeing. One practical reason is that eating foods that naturally grow in your area maximizes your chances of obtaining and eating them fresh. Imported foods require long-haul transportation and possibly, either they're no longer as fresh or have been treated with preservatives. Neither of which leads to optimal health and wellbeing.

The Spiritual Component of Food

Particularly in western medicine, the primary belief is that food is purely physiological in nature. As such, it only looks at the physical impact or benefits of eating. Interestingly enough, a study showed the possibility that eating food may also have a spiritual or emotional aspect to it.

The study fed two groups of people the same meal, i.e., one loaded with cholesterol, sugar, salt, and saturated fats. The first group eats their meal in a noisy environment with lots of traffic and construction activities going on around them. The other group ate their meal in a relatively quiet place with gentle sounds and music playing in the background. Afterward, the researchers took the participants' blood pressures and triglyceride levels.

The findings were unexpected - at least for those who merely considered the physiological aspect of food. The food given to the participants was obviously harmful in terms of both blood pressure and triglyceride levels, but the results were different.

Both indicators rose in subjects who ate their meals in a very noisy environment. But both indicators for those who ate their meals in a relatively quiet environment went down. While this may not be very conclusive, it shows that the effects of food on the body may not necessarily depend completely on its physiological characteristics and nutrient profiles. A person's mental or emotional state, which may be influenced or affected by the eating environment, may also play a significant role.

Based on this study, there's more to our health and wellbeing than simply what we eat. It's highly possible that the way we interact with our food matters as well. To this extent, it is very important to have the right attitude when eating food. An attitude of gratitude may also be crucial to get the most benefits from the foods we eat.

Eating Properly for Adequate Qi

What are the best foods for optimal qi flow in your body? A generally healthy diet is naturally good for your qi. To optimize the latter, certain types of food are needed.

One guiding principle in choosing qi flow-optimizing food and drinks is the glycemic index, e.g., GI. This refers to the ability of the food you consume to raise blood sugar levels rapidly; specifically, the impact on the body's insulin response. All food and drinks lie within a spectrum between low glycemic index and high glycemic index.

The low glycemic index or low GI foods take time to break down in the stomach and be converted to glucose. As such, they don't immediately flood the bloodstream with glucose, and as a result, blood sugar levels remain relatively steady and minimize insulin production.

On the other end of the spectrum, high GI foods are those that are easily broken down and converted to glucose. As a result, glucose quickly enters the bloodstream and triggers greater insulin production.

Now, what's the deal about blood sugar levels and insulin production? When you eat a lot of foods high on the glycemic index, your blood sugar levels become very volatile. Then your blood sugar spikes and crashes which is its trademark.

Have you ever felt so energetic after downing a large serving of soda only to feel lethargic or even sleepy shortly thereafter? That happens when your blood sugar levels become volatile. When glucose quickly enters your bloodstream, it spikes up your blood sugar and makes you feel as if you have high energy. After your pancreas senses the sugar spike, it'll quickly produce lots of insulin to counteract it.

However, the problem with the pancreas is that it's not able to properly estimate the right amount of insulin needed to normalize blood sugar. As a result, it usually produces a lot of insulin to overcorrect your high blood sugar levels, dropping them below normal. Often called sugar crashes, this makes you feel lethargic or sleepy. When this happens, your body starts to intensely crave high GI foods again to bring blood sugar levels back to normal quickly. Then, the cycle continues. Blood sugar spikes again and crashes again, giving you that energetic then suddenly lethargic feeling all over again.

But when you eat mostly low glycemic index foods or carbohydrates, you enjoy the benefit of relatively steady blood sugar levels. This means they neither spike nor crash, which gives you a steady dose of energy throughout the day. This ability to consistently release energy into your system makes it an ideal food for the Qigong diet.

Some of the best sources of low GI or complex carbohydrates include whole-grain foods:

1. Barley

2. Brown rice

3. Buckwheat

4. Oatmeal

5. Quinoa

6. Sweet potatoes

7. Whole wheat bread

8. Foods made primarily of whole grain flour, such as pasta and noodles

Carbohydrates aren't necessarily one of two extremes, low and high GI. They may also lie between, i.e., mid glycemic index. If you have no choice but to eat mid or high GI carbohydrates, you can lower their glycemic index by eating them with protein and healthy dietary fats. This slows down their digestion and, ultimately, their conversion to glucose.

And speaking of proteins, the best ones for a Qigong-friendly diet are organic sources of white meat. Being organic, they don't contain GMO substances and/or steroids. White meat is preferred because, typically, they contain very little or no facts.

But of course, not everyone can afford organic food. That's why focusing mostly on white meat isn't just important but also practical. These include turkey or chicken breast.

Other excellent proteins and healthy dietary fat sources are seafood such as tuna, salmon, sardines, and cod. You may also get these from eggs, organic if possible. However, you must limit your weekly consumption of these foods.

Some excellent protein sources include tofu, legumes, rice milk, soya milk, and soy yogurt to go vegetarian or vegan.

Consistent with traditional Chinese medicine principles, a healthy, Qigong-friendly diet includes a lot of vegetables. If you can afford to, go for organic and locally grown ones. They're both pesticide-free and are as fresh as possible. The best way to eat them is raw. If you prefer to eat them cooked, steaming or stir-frying them is ideal. Other excellent plant sources of key nutrients include seeds, nuts, beans, and soya bean curd or tofu.

Two other excellent plant foods to include in a Qigong-based diet are kelp and nori. Both are made from seaweed and contain lots of phytonutrients, especially antioxidants.

Last, try not to microwave your food or, at the very least, limit them. Doing this depletes your foods available qi.

For a Qigong-based diet, there are two main types of foods you need to include as much as possible: qi-building and deficiency-reducing. Some of the best qi-building foods include:

1. Almonds

2. Apples

3. Asparagus

4. Barley

5. Beef

6. Berries

7. Black sesame seeds

8. Buckwheat

9. Button mushrooms

10. Cabbages

11. Cheese

12. cherries

13. Chicken (especially breast)

14. Chicken liver

15. Coconuts

16. Corn

17. Dates

18. Duck

19. Eel

20. Eggplants

21. Figs

22. Goose

23. Ham

24. Herring

25. Honey

26. Lamb

27. Lentils

28. Logans

29. Mackerel

30. Malt

31. Milk

32. Mussels

33. Oats

34. Octopi

35. Oysters

36. Peanuts

37. Potatoes

38. Rice syrup

39. Rice

40. Squash

41. Sweet potatoes

42. Tomatoes

43. Trout

44. Tunas

45. Turkey (especially breast)

46. Walnuts

47. Wheat bran

48. Yam

49. Yogurt

50. Supplements such as pollen, royal jelly, algae, and ginseng

Excellent foods for rectifying qi deficiencies include:

1. Apples
2. Beef
3. Cherries
4. Chicken
5. Dates
6. Figs
7. Goose meat
8. Ham
9. Lamb
10. Licorice
11. Loganberries
12. Molasses
13. Oats
14. Rice
15. Squash
16. Sweet potatoes
17. Sweet rice
18. Tofu
19. Yams
20. Supplements like pollen, algae, royal jelly, and American ginseng

And to ensure optimal qi through your diet, avoid or minimize these types of foods:

1. Artificial flavorings
2. Food coloring
3. High-glycemic index carbs (sugar-loaded foods) like soda, juices, raw sugars, candies, cakes, etc.

4. Refined, processed, and/or canned foods

5. Synthetic preservatives

6. White bread

7. White flour

8. White rice

Chapter 10: A Daily Qigong Routine

For your daily practice, it's important to remember that Qigong isn't just a physical practice but a mental one as well. Every Qigong session involves the following physical and mental aspects:

1. Calming down the mind and focusing your intention

2. Right postures that facilitate the free flow of your energy

3. Controlling your breath to stimulate your qi and body

4. Being aware of your energy or qi

Before anything else, let's talk about awareness levels first. You see, qigong exercises provide benefits on different levels. These include:

1. Stretching, working, and loosening joints and muscles in your body

2. Coordination of your movements with your breath

3. Creation and storage of qi or energy in the Dantian, which helps you learn to balance the body relative to forces of the exercises' movements and gravity

4. Giving your internal organs and their connecting nerves a healthy massage

5. Stimulation of energy flow through your medians related to the organs

Because of these, being aware of your energy or qi involves different levels, which include:

1. Awareness of the sensations in your spine, joints, and muscles while performing the movements

2. Awareness of each breath's stretching and releasing effects on your movements

3. Awareness of your Dantian

4. Awareness of the internal massage for your organs

5. Awareness of how your qi or energy is flowing with your meridian

To develop awareness, learn just a few exercises at a time. When you are comfortable and aware of how each movement feels, start adding one or two exercises to your daily sessions. Continue adding the others until you can practice them all comfortably. You must know completely how the movements feel in your spine, joints, and muscles.

Once you've developed an awareness of the sensations of the movements, it's time to work on becoming aware of your breathing and, more importantly, its stretching and releasing effects during your exercise movements. One way to do this is by coordinating your breath with the movements. For example, exhale when the movement involves moving your limbs away from your body and inhaling as you move them back towards it.

Once you have become aware of your breath and how it impacts your movements, the next level is awareness of your Dantian. In particular, it's about being mindful of how your body expands and contracts around it.

Next, it's time to work on developing awareness of specific organs and being internally massaged during your exercise sessions. Your ability to do this can help you learn how to perform the Qigong exercises in the right sequence based on the time of the day.

Last, you also need to be aware of how your qi or energy flows along specific meridians. This can be challenging at first because awareness can be quite subtle. Over time and with constant practice, you'll be able to feel it more and more.

Remember that developing all levels of awareness is more of a marathon than a race or a sprint. Take your time developing each awareness level one at a time, and by doing this, instead of jumping the learning curve by working on all levels simultaneously, you'll be able to establish a solid foundation for your daily Qigong exercise routines.

Remember that the exercises need to be performed with minimum muscular tension (positions that are as relaxed as possible) and in slow, flowing movements. The slower your movements, the more beneficial they can be.

However, it's also important to remember that your Qigong practice shouldn't feel strained or uncomfortable. Hence, go as slow as comfortably possible. When it becomes uncomfortable, you're probably doing it too slow and, thus, may need to increase the speed slightly.

Initially, don't worry if you're unable to move as slow as seasoned practitioners. As a beginner, it's normal. Gradually slow down your movements during several days, weeks, or even months as you regularly perform them. Eventually, you'll be able to develop the necessary fitness and stamina to go as slow as possible and maximize the benefits of regular Qigong exercise.

Again, don't rush your movements to complete the required number of repetitions of your exercises quickly. If you're pressed for time, prioritize comfort over the need to finish your target repetitions at all costs. The key is to perform the movements in a relaxed and flowing manner. When you force yourself to finish a specific number of reps within a limited amount of time, you may end up performing them improperly, rushing the movements, and forfeiting much of the exercises' benefits.

Before we go to the exercises themselves, you must know that if your personal circumstances or physical condition makes standing exercises very difficult or impossible, you may perform them sitting down with minor modifications to the movements. The ideal sitting position is one where you're on the edge of a bench, chair, or stool and at a height that allows your thighs/hamstrings to be as parallel as possible to the floor. Sitting this way helps you ensure proper posture for your spine during the exercises.

Sitting this way also helps you learn to assume the horse stance or ma bu excellently. It also helps maximize the stretching effect on your spine, which, in turn, can help you improve flexibility in your lower back muscles. Eventually, it can make assuming the standing horse stance with your pelvis tucked under much easier.

Awareness of Energy

The most important benefit associated with Qigong exercises is optimal development and circulation of the qi or energy throughout your body. The earlier you recognize and actually feel this energy, the quicker your progress can be.

When trying to become aware of your qi, you'll experience several sensations. One of the most common feelings is that of two opposite poles of a magnet being drawn together or being pushed apart. Another one is a warm fuzzy feeling. Others note, feeling it tinkling or breeze-like sensation on their skin. As you continue with your Qigong journey, you will likely experience these sensations and probably more.

It's possible that from the get-go, you may already start to feel them. It may also take you some time. Regardless, the important thing is to acknowledge those sensations as they come. Neither force nor convince yourself to feel sensations that aren't really there. Just be consistent in practicing these exercises, and in time, you become aware of your qi.

The moment you become aware of feeling your energy, you can develop it regardless of how subtle it is. Over time and with regular practice, you learn to use your mind to direct your qi to the specific areas of your body and, eventually, increase your recognition and sensitivity to them.

At first, you'll likely be most aware of the qi in your hands. Why? It's because it's one of the body parts that you tend to be most aware of, considering how frequently you use them to hold, feel, and use things. Also, there are a lot of nerve endings in your hands, and blood flows to them easily compared to other body parts.

With continuous practice, you'll feel the energy start to develop in your arms and ultimately develop in your legs until you feel it all over your body.

A very practical way to start developing awareness of your energy is by doing this simple exercise:

1. Clap your hands robustly and intermittently for at least one minute. You should feel a warm and possibly tingling sensation in your hands by the time you stop clapping. This is a positive sign because all that clapping helps stimulate the nerve endings in your hands, resulting in increased blood flow in said area. Remember, qi flow is closely linked to blood flow and nervous system functioning; hence the tingling sensation makes you aware of your energy.

2. Now, join your hands in front of you but just short of touching. As you do this and hold the position, you'll be able to feel a warm sensation between your hands because of all that clapping.

3. Next, start moving your hands in and out slightly first by bringing them close together (not touching) then pulling them far apart enough you can still feel the warmth between your hands.

4. As you continue doing this, gradually increase the distance between your hands. Over time and with enough practice, you'll start feeling something similar to a magnetic push or pull between your hands while moving them.

5. While increasing the distance between your hands when pulling them apart, imagine a warm sphere of magnetic energy pushing back against your hands and growing. As you bring them closer together, think about squeezing that ball.

6. Always remember to breathe.

While many people can start feeling their qi the first time they do this exercise, others don't. If you're one of the latter, don't worry. With consistent practice, you should be able to feel it, too. Coupling this exercise, together with the other ones in this chapter, helps increase your awareness and your ability to control your qi.

Here are some exercises to help increase your awareness of your qi.

String Pulling

1. Begin by standing with a relaxed posture.

2. In your mind's eye, see a ring between your feet just in front of you.

3. Visualize a piece of string passing through the said ring, with one end tied to your left middle finger and the other two you're right middle finger.

4. As you start lifting your right hand. As you do, move your left hand down towards the direction of the imaginary ring. It should feel as though the ring is some kind of pulley through which your imaginary string passes through in that as you pull one hand up, it pulls the other one down towards the ring.

5. Pull your left hand upward and in the process, imagine that the string attached to your left middle finger is pulling your right hand down towards the ring.

6. Feel the pull of the string in one hand on the other as you alternately lift each hand.

Another way to perform this exercise is by replacing the imaginary string with an imaginary energy column instead. One end of this column is attached to your left hand and the other to your right hand. Like the imaginary string, imagine passing through a fixed point on the floor between your feet. As with the string, imagine one hand being pulled down as the other is raised alternately.

Wall Pushes

1. Begin by standing straight and close to a wall.

2. Raise both hands in front of you such that your arms are perpendicular to your torso.

3. Move your hands very close to the wall, but not touching it, before moving them away from it.

4. Every time you bring your hands very close to the wall, feel the energy between them being compressed. Doing this helps you feel a magnetic force pushing back against your hands as you compress them against the wall.

The Energy Ball

1. Begin by moving your hands close together until you start to feel an energy ball between them.

2. Next, start moving your hands in a round motion just like you would when rubbing around a basketball, a soccer ball, or any kind of ball.

3. As you continue moving your hands in a circular motion, gradually increase the distance between them while continuing to feel the sensation of rubbing the energy ball's surface.

4. Wait for your energy ball to expand to your desired size. At this point, start squeezing it while continuing the circular motion of your hands. Doing this may make you feel the energy ball heating up and warming your hands. You may also feel an increasing magnetic feel and the ball becoming heavier.

An Overview of Your Qigong Sessions

Each Qigong session comprises three important aspects: the warm-up, the exercises, and the cool-down. You can refer to chapter 7 for the warm-up exercises.

For the exercise proper itself, you must perform them in order based on what time of the day you're practicing. You may begin with ones linked to organs whose peak activities coincide with the time of the day you're doing Qigong exercises. Then, perform the other exercises according to their peak activity time, ending your sessions back with exercises linked to the organ that's currently at peak activity.

Pay close attention to how you feel and your breathing throughout your Qigong sessions. Should you feel dizzy, short of breath, or very uncomfortable at any point, stop for a while and take a break. Let a minute or two passed by so your energy and breathing normalize before resuming your session.

At the end of your workout, start the cool-down process. Place both hands on the base of your abdomen, just in front of your Dantian. Feel the energy in it and pay close attention to your breathing, which must be slow and steady.

Continue cooling down by massaging different parts of your body related to your meridians' energy flow directions. Do this by patting, rubbing, or running your hands along the surface of your body. Do this towards the direction of your meridians but without touching it. By doing this, you can facilitate energy distribution all over your body to help you feel refreshed and stimulated.

You can cap off the cool-down process by putting your hands back on top of your lower abs. As you do this, become aware of your Dantian and your breathing again for a few minutes.

As you end your Qigong routine, it's important to properly cool down as with any form of exercise. Here are some exercises for ending your sessions properly.

The Energy Massage

1. Start by standing street with feet about shoulder-width apart and both hands resting on your lower belly. While in this position, take your time and be aware of your breath and your Dantian.

2. Next, pull your hands apart and place them on your lower back. Gradually, run them down the sides of your lower body, starting from the lower back to your hips, calves, and feet.

3. Place your hands on the insides of your feet. Move them up the inside of your calves and thighs. Then, put your hands in front of your stomach and run them upward to your chest.

4. Extend your left arm to the side, then run your right hand along its inside, starting from the shoulder all the way to the left hand.

5. Next, turn your left arm over and run back your right hand along the outside of the arm, passing over the elbow, until it returns back to your right chest.

6. Bring your left hand back to your left chest and extend the right hand to the side.

7. Run your left hand along the inside of your right arm, starting from the shoulder all the way to the hand.

8. Turn over your right arm and run your left hand back along the outside of the arm until it goes back to the left chest.

9. With both hands now in front of your chest, run them both along your face and up your head. Continue running them down your nape, shoulders, and behind your waist.

10. This constitutes one repetition. You may repeat this as often as you want.

11. To end this massage, bring both hands back to your lower stomach. Bring your focus back to your breathing and your Dantian.

Benefit Specific Qigong Routines

The routines above help you experience the many health and wellbeing benefits of Qigong. If you want shorter sessions that focus on specific benefits, here are some daily routines you can try.

Vitality Routine

This one helps stimulate most of your acupuncture meridians and internal organs and invigorate your body. Here's how to do it:

1. Start by assuming a comfortable, grounded standing position, with feet about shoulder-width or slightly wider than shoulder-width apart. Let your arms hang on the sides.

2. Take a few deep breaths, inhaling through the nose and exhaling through the mouth. Be aware of your breathing.

3. Start the routine by bringing your arms sideward-up over your head in an elliptical manner. Inhale deeply while doing this.

4. Bring your hands down the front-middle of your body. Lower your body by squatting slightly until your hands are in front of your thighs. Exhale as you do this.

5. Raise your hands and arms in an elliptical motion. Stop when both of your hands are at the top of your head. Inhale as you do this.

6. Repeat the last two steps 5-6 times.

7. Assume the starting position with feet about shoulder-width apart or slightly wider, with arms relaxed on your side.

8. Keeping your arms limp, swing them like pendulums from side to side by moving your weight sideways. It's like performing multiple golf swings in opposite directions in successive fashion, but with limp arms. Perform this movement 10 to 20 times.

9. Next, raise your arms and hands in front of your body up to chest level, with palms facing each other while you inhale. Keeping arms extended, move them as far back as possible without discomfort to open your torso/chest. Continue inhaling.

10. Close your chest by moving your arms forward until your hands are in front of your middle chest but not touching each other while exhaling. With palms facing down, bring your arms down while squatting slightly until your hands are at mid-thigh level. Continue exhaling at this point.

11. Repeat steps 9 and 10 ten times.

12. Go back to the starting position, but with a wider than shoulder-width stance and toes pointed outward at roughly 45 degrees.

13. Breathe in while bringing your extended arms up – palms facing the sky – in front of your body while breathing in. Once your hands are at eye level, turn your palms over and bring the arms down until the hands are at waist level while squatting and exhaling. The lowest you should squat is the point where your knees are in a vertical line with your toes or when it starts to feel too strenuous, whichever comes first.

14. Turn your palms up and raise your arms until the hands are at eye level while standing back up and inhaling deeply.

15. Repeat steps 13 and 14 ten times.

16. Go back to the starting position.

17. Bring your palms in front of your belly, facing up. Breathe in deeply while bringing them up to chest level.

18. Turn your palms over and push them down up to the crotch area while exhaling.

19. Repeat steps 17 & 18 ten times.

20. Go back to the starting position and take several deep breaths to end.

Stress Relief, Energy, and Vitality Routine

1. Start by assuming a comfortable, grounded standing position, with feet about shoulder-width or slightly wider than shoulder-width apart. Let your arms hang on the sides.

2. Take a few deep breaths, inhaling through the nose and exhaling through the mouth. Be aware of your breathing.

3. Start the routine by bringing your arms sideward-up over your head in an elliptical manner. Inhale deeply while doing these.

4. Bring your hands down the middle-front of your body with palms facing down. Lower your body slightly squatting until your hands are in front of your thighs. Exhale as you do this.

5. Raise your hands and arms in an elliptical motion. Stop at the top of your head. Inhale as you do these.

6. Repeat the last two steps 5-6 times.

7. Assume the starting position.

8. Breathe in as you bring your hands up the middle-front of your body. Stop when they're above your head.

9. Bring your hands down in an elliptical motion while exhaling. Simultaneously, squat slightly until your hands are in front of your thighs. They should be slightly below crotch level.

10. While inhaling and standing back up, raise your hands back up along the center of your body.

11. Repeat steps 8 to 10 ten times.

12. Go back to the starting position, but with a slightly wider than shoulder-width stance this time. Extend your right hand to your side and make a big circle with it in front of your body. Your palms should face the direction of the movement.

13. During the downward phase of the circle, slightly lunge toward the movement. During the sideward movement at the bottom portion of the circle, shift your lunge to the other side. Stand back up during the upward phase of the motion.

14. Repeat steps 12 to 13 ten times before doing another ten repetitions with the other hand.

15. Go back to the starting position with a normal, shoulder-width stance.

16. Turn to the right side with your right foot forward and the left one planted at a 45-degree angle at the back. Your hips must face the right side.

17. Extend your arms in front of your chest, palms closely facing each other and fingers pointing forward.

18. Breathe in as you draw your palms to your chest and fingers pointing upwards, e.g., praying hands. As you do this, move backward by shifting your body weight to your hind leg, i.e., the left one. Keep both feet planted on the ground.

19. With palms still facing each other, draw the largest circle you can with them. As you bring them down along the center of your body and raising them as far forward as you can up to chest level, breathe out. Shift your body weight forward to your right leg as you do this.

20. As you draw your palms towards your chest, shift your weight backward to your left leg and breathe in.

21. Repeat steps 17 to 20 ten times before doing the same with the left leg in front and the right one behind.

22. Go back to the starting position, with feet shoulder-width apart.

23. Start by shifting your weight to the left side of your body, with your right hand raised to the left side of your face, about 6 inches away. Put your left hand down your left side.

24. Shift your body weight to the right in a sliding manner, with your right leg now supporting it. Keep both feet planted on the ground. As you do, slide your left hand to the front of your right hip and reposition your right hand to the left side of your face, the palm facing it. Inhale while doing this.

25. Switch hand positions, i.e., bring your left hand up to the right side of your face and your right hand down on the right side of your body. Shift your body weight in a sliding motion back to the left, sliding your right hand to the front of your left hip, and repositioning your left hand to the left side of your face. Exhale while doing this.

26. Repeat steps 23-25 ten to twenty times.

27. Assume the starting position but with arms as if you're hugging a tree. Keep fingers an inch apart, and your knees slightly bent. Breathe deeply and naturally while drawing qi from the earth. Keep your body relaxed with as little tension as possible to keep your arms up as long as possible. Hold the position for as long as comfortably possible.

Tips to Maximize Your Qigong Routine Benefits

To enjoy the benefits of Qigong practice, consistency is of utmost importance. If you want to maximize them, you can supplement them with other practices. The following are some ways to do this.

Preparation

As cliche as it sounds, "failing to plan is planning to fail" has a great deal of truth to it. As another saying goes, what gets scheduled gets done.

Adequate preparation involves blocking off time for your regular Qigong practice. It doesn't just happen; naturally, you have to make time for it. If you're a morning person, considering sleeping early so you can wake up earlier and make time for Qigong. Or if you're more of an evening person, try to end your day earlier so you'll have enough time to do it at night just before you go to bed. If you're neither, consider using your lunch break to do this in a quiet and private area at work.

Another aspect of preparation is energy management. This means eating healthy foods in the right amounts and getting enough sleep. As you learned earlier in the chapter on the Qigong diet, eat lower GI, complex carbs, lean protein, and healthy fats. Doing so will help you enjoy steady energy throughout the day so you can consistently practice Qigong on top of your other daily duties.

There is no specific benchmark for how many hours you need every night for sleep because each person is different. On average, you may need anywhere between seven to nine hours of sleep at night for optimal energy throughout the day. The best way you can estimate your nightly sleep requirements yes by sleeping at the same time at night and not waking up with an alarm. Start a sleeping journal, and on it, take note of how many hours of sleep you got the previous night, and more importantly, how you felt the next day. After about a week or two of sleep journaling, you'll be able to get an idea of your personal sleep requirements.

Another way to sleep optimally is by adjusting your sleeping or waking hours according to the average sleep cycle, which is about 90 minutes or 1-1/2 hours. Using this cycle, you can either determine what time to sleep based on your wake-up time or adjust the latter based on the time you want to sleep at night. A very useful app for this is sleep time, which is an android app. If your wake-up time is non-negotiable, you can type it in the app, and it will tell you what hours are best for you to hit the sack. If you have more leeway in terms of waking up in the morning, you can type in the time you want to sleep, and it will show you the best times to wake up per the 90-minute sleep cycle.

Patience

We live in a world that seeks to get results as fast as possible, hence the reference to a microwave society. However, the best things in life often take time to accomplish or experience. The awesome health and wellbeing benefits of Qigong are among those.

Instead of focusing on the benefits themselves, make developing Qigong into a habit your primary goal. By doing so, you'll be less pressured to reap the benefits quickly, and chances are, it will be easier for you to slow down and enjoy the practice itself. If you successfully develop this habit, regular practice will no longer be a struggle, and the benefits will automatically and consistently come.

But if you hurry things up, you're increasing the likelihood of being unable to experience Qigong's benefits. For one, trying to speed up the process can lead to overexertion. In turn, this can lead to burnout, injuries, or worse, both.

Remember, Rome wasn't built in a day, but they were busy laying bricks by the hour. Experiencing optimal health and wellbeing through Qigong takes time, but it'll be worth the wait.

Find Your Why

Last, you must have a compelling reason for engaging in Qigong and making it a regular part of your life. Without one, you'll likely give up once things become inconvenient or even hard. If you have a very compelling reason for wanting to practice it, you'll find enough strength and fortitude to continue even when the going gets rough.

While it's good to pursue Qigong for optimal health and wellbeing, I don't think it's compelling enough for most people. Why? It's a very general or vague motivation. It's not personal enough. A more compelling reason related to health and wellbeing could be not wanting to be a burden to the family because of sickness and disease. Another one is enjoying as many years as possible with your spouse. In other words, your reasons for engaging in the practice should be something very personal and can be achieved with optimal health and well-being.

Qigong Exercises

Qi Locks

These are hand positions required in some of the Qigong exercises. They're meant to help keep your qi or energy flowing within your body and prevent it from leaking out.

The first qi lock resembles a fist, only that the thumb is inside the four fingers instead of covering them. This is a very useful type of qi lock because many of your meridians end with the fingertips.

Since this position brings all the fingers of your hand inward to your palm, it allows you to build up qi and keep it flowing inside your body.

Another qi lock used in the exercises is called the crane's head. You lock your hands by bringing all five fingertips of your hand together. This helps facilitate optimal qi circulation and keeps it from leaking.

Conclusion

Qigong is one of the best investments you can make that can help you live an optimally healthy, joy-filled, and satisfying life. Practicing it daily doesn't cost a penny. It's not as strenuous as most other forms of exercise, and most importantly, its benefits can be truly life-changing. Now that you have read this book, you are in a great position to start practicing it and be on your way to an optimally healthy and vigorous life.

However, the knowledge you've gained here is just potential power. To unleash its true power, you must practice what you've learned as soon as possible. The longer you procrastinate, the higher your risks of not doing the practice and, ultimately, missing out on the kind of life it can give.

Hence, practice what you've learned immediately. Remember, you don't have to practice everything all at once. Just start with one or two exercises and take baby steps first. That way, you already start moving the needle at a pace that will not lead to burnout. Baby steps are more likely to be consistent, and Qigong's benefits require consistency. So, better to start taking small steps now than none at all.

Here's to your health and wellbeing, my friend!

Part 2: Tai Chi

Unlocking the Power of an Internal Chinese Martial Art, Including the 24 Forms and Meditation Techniques for Beginners

Introduction

Tai Chi is an age-old practice used to calm the mind and body. It is a sequence of different movements, postures, and forms that require you to maintain focus. Tai Chi is an internal martial art and can be used in combat. Through Tai Chi, you learn to harness your qi and the energy around you to defeat your opponent. If you have watched the movie *Mulan*, you know how she uses her qi to defeat the Huns.

Tai Chi is about using breath and other meditative techniques to relax your mind and control energy flow. You can practice its different movements while you sit, walk, stand or move. You may need to adapt the movements, so you can perform them in different situations.

If you are new to Tai Chi, you can use this book as your guide. In this book, you will first be introduced to Tai Chi to give you a brief history of this martial art. You will then look at its philosophy and principles, which are extremely important for you to know if you want to become a Tai Chi practitioner. You will then move on to how Tai Chi benefits your physical, spiritual, mental, and emotional wellbeing. There is a lot of research being conducted to determine how the art reduces the risk of developing certain illnesses and diseases, and you will look at these as well.

Since Tai Chi is an internal martial art, it focuses on breathing and meditation to help you focus and manage energy. You learn to harness your qi and use it to maintain different postures and movements. It is only when you master this that you can balance your body in any position. This book has all the information you need about Tai Chi meditation and the different techniques you can use to switch into the meditative state. You will also learn strategies and tips to defeat your opponent if you were to fight.

The book also provides information on the different movements and stances used in Tai Chi. It has instructions and illustrations to help you master the movements. Since Tai Chi is not a fun sport, it can be difficult for you to stick to it. This book has several tips you can use to help you persevere with the art and improve over time. It is best to work with people you know to maintain discipline.

Hopefully, you will learn more about Tai Chi and master the different forms and movements used. Thank you for choosing this book. You should find it informative in your quest to learn Tai Chi.

Chapter 1: What is Tai Chi?

Tai Chi is an art that helps you to learn to embrace the mind, spirit, and body. This art originated in ancient China, and it is an effective exercise routine that helps you maintain the health of your body and mind. It requires a great depth of skill and knowledge to practice the art, but it is easy to learn and embrace the benefits. Most people continue to use this art throughout their lives.

There are different forms of Tai Chi, and the major ones will be discussed later in the book. Every style has a different feature, while the principles of each style remain the same. Some essential principles include the following:

- Integrating the mind with the body
- Controlling movements and breath
- Generating energy internally
- Being mindful
- Loosening the muscles
- Being serene

The objective of Tai Chi is to help you cultivate the life energy or qi found within the human body to make sure the energy flows powerfully and smoothly throughout the body. It is only possible to maintain total harmony between the outer and inner selves by integrating the body and mind. You can maintain this balance by empowering yourself through the practice of qi. There are modern Tai Chi programs that incorporate medical science, and these programs will deliver benefits faster.

There is much more to Tai Chi than one may initially believe. Not many understand the art because they cannot describe it easily in a sentence. This art is enjoyable, aesthetically pleasing, and easy to practice. Tai Chi is part meditation and part-integral exercise for the parts of the mind and body. This art can help you think clearly but bear in mind that it can be a different experience for you. It is best to practice the art regularly if you want to benefit from it to the maximum.

When you perform Tai Chi, you realize that every flowing movement you make has immense inner strength. The movements are like the water in a river. Beneath the surface of the river, there is an underlying current, which has immense power. This power can heal you and improve your wellbeing. When you practice Tai Chi consistently, you will feel the internal energy and learn to convert that energy into an internal force that allows you to generate more internal energy. This process enhances the development of Tai Chi, which leads to a balanced physical and mental state. Your balance and agility also improve. Tai Chi focuses on helping you build inner strength. This means you can begin practicing Tai Chi at any age.

Research shows that Tai Chi improves flexibility, immunity, strength, and fitness, relieves pain, and increases your wellbeing. You will look at these benefits in detail in the subsequent chapter. Your muscles need to become strong if you want to protect and support your joints. Strong muscles are also important to maintain normal physical function. Through flexibility exercises, you will move easily and improve the circulation of blood and fluid throughout your body. This improves healing. You also need to be fit if you want to maintain the health of your muscles, heart, and lungs. Movements in Tai Chi ensure you transfer weight equally from one part of your body to another, enabling you to maintain balance.

Tai Chi is more than the health benefits it has to offer. It is extremely easy to learn, and most people who practice Tai Chi make it a way of life. Since Tai Chi is a very deep subject, there is nobody who knows everything about Tai Chi. The subject is fascinating, and many want to embark on the journey. When you practice Tai Chi, you enter a state of tranquility and move into a different space, world, and time. You do not have to hustle or maintain a schedule in this world. This is a spiritual experience. These types of experiences are satisfying beyond words.

History of Tai Chi

The story of Tai Chi starts with Buddha. It begins with the beginning of Zen and ancient old times in 600 BC. Jia Ye was the only person who knew why Buddha picked up a lotus flower during a meeting and smiled at everyone. He was a great disciple and smiled back at Buddha because he understood the meaning. This was when Buddha told everybody on Mount Lengjia, "I have a treasure, like a secret mountain, which is real but with not any appearance, now I give it to JiaYe the Great." The treasure was to be passed between people, which was the case when families passed the treasure and learning of Zen from one generation to the next.

Buddhism in India began to decay after the Zen was passed on to the DaMo, which was the tenth generation. So, DaMo went to China during the Liang dynasty. He went to the Shao-Lin temple and settled down there. The Emperor of the Liang dynasty went to meet DaMo. It was then that DaMo developed methods of training that helped people develop inner peace. He trained a person's soul and body. Another one of his contributions was the development of another form of fighting called Shao-Lin Kung Fu. This is where the student learns to fight using his spirit. Shao-Lin Kung Fu led to the beginning of the Tang dynasty.

One of the founders of Taoism, Lao-Tzu, was alive at the same time as Buddha. Lao-Tzu was a famous Chinese philosopher, and he developed the theory of Yin and Yang. When he developed this theory, he described the relationship between nature and man. He also talked about the relationship between the strong and weak. Confucius once said he was a dragon. His paper "Tao-Te Ching" was valued greatly by people for many years. In this paper, he talked about how one should learn from nature since nature is everybody's first teacher. He also said, "The newborn baby is weak and soft, but the growing force is strong. When he grows up, he becomes strong and stiff, and the life strength is weak and soft. When something is overwhelmed, it is near its end, although it looks strong." These words have influenced Tai Chi since it is close to Taoism. After Lao-Tzu developed this form of Tai Chi, there were numerous training methods developed in China that aimed to combine the forces of nature and people.

There were different forms of physical practices used in China, and in each of these styles, many people, including Wang Chongyang in Zhongnan Mountain, Xu Xuanping in the Sung Dynasty, and Chang Sanfeng, the founder of Tai-Chi Chuan, learned everything they needed to from nature. They learned to pay attention to every thought and breath. They also focused on how their minds began to change. They learned from outer appearances and learned the meaning of the different natural phenomena.

India Yoga school methods, Taoism methods, and Buddhism methods used traditional and oriental training styles, which are different from modern learning methods. These skills are different from bodybuilding and jogging. These forms of exercise are easy ways to solve different problems in life.

Beginning of Tai Chi

Chinese Kung Fu was developed and created in the Buddhism temple called Shao-Lin. This was where most people went to learn Kung Fu. Chang Sanfeng also learned Kung Fu in this temple before traveling across China to learn more about Taoism. He settled down in the Wudang Mountains. Since he was a recluse and a well-respected master, many people went to him to learn martial arts. This form of martial arts is termed Wudang Chuan. Shao-Lin and Wudang are the major forms of Kung Fu styles. One of these forms, the Wudang form, is a form of inner Kung Fu.

Wudang began Tai Chi in his later years, and he did not teach this skill publicly. It was an esoteric technique that was passed on from one generation to the next. Some Tai Chi skills were passed on, but most of them were left unknown to the public.

Modern Tai Chi

Modern Tai Chi began close to 400 years ago. Now you will look at a few styles that developed during this phase.

Chen School of Tai Chi

After the Ming dynasty fell and decayed over time, Chen Wangting moved back to his village. He began to study the art of Kung Fu. Since he was a warrior and general, he was closely connected with Shao Lin. This allowed him to learn more about the various styles of Kung Fu. He knew the different methods and theories used in this form of martial arts. He compiled and developed a version of Kung Fu in his village, which focused only on inner values and peace.

Wang School of Tai Chi

Wang Zongyue developed this style of Tai Chi. He was a recluse in his village and theorized various aspects of Tai Chi. People believed that Wang carried the skill of Tai Chi, which was a gift given to him by Chang Sanfeng. He was very skilled at fighting and taught children how to defend themselves. Some historians theorized that Wang taught the theory of Tai Chi to the people in Chen's village. He passed on different forms of martial arts, including Tai Chi, to the people in Chen's village. It was only 60 years after his death that his paper on Tai Chi was discovered in Wuyang County. This led to the development of the Wushi Tai Chi school.

Chen's School to Yang's School of Tai Chi

Yang LuChan, one of the greatest masters of Tai Chi, had gone to Chen's village to learn this martial art when he was young. Since the skill was kept a secret by the people in the village, he pretended to be a beggar. He used to learn martial arts in secret when he worked in the village. When the people in the village discovered what he was doing, they convinced the head of the village to change the rules. They allowed people from other parts of China to come to the village to learn more about this skill.

Wushi School of Tai Chi

Wushi Xiang was a rich landlord. He preferred Kung Fu and practiced this art regularly. He was amicable and made friends easily. Wushi befriended Yang when he came back from Chen's village. Since Wushi loved martial arts, he admired Yang's movements, but he could not learn everything from Yang. Wushi then went to Chen's village to learn the art of Tai Chi. Because the head of the village had died, not many people in the village taught the art of Tai Chi. He then wandered until he came across a member from Chen's village, Chen ChingPing, who taught the skill there. Wu also learned the art of Tai Chi from the paper written by Wang. This was published when it was found in the salt shop.

Wu School of Tai Chi

The Wu style was developed by Wu Quanyou, one of the Imperial Guard members during the Ching dynasty. Wu had mastered Kung Fu before he learned the art of Tai Chi. Wu took care of Yang Luchan when he fell ill because he respected the skill. Since Wu took care of Yang, they became good friends, and Yang was indebted to Wu. Yang taught Wu the skill of Tai Chi in return for his favor. After his death, Yang asked his son Yang Banhou to teach Wu. When he mastered the art of Tai Chi, he used his understanding of both Kung Fu and Tai Chi to develop a new style that became known as Wu. His style is slow, soft, and calm. The style required people to pay attention to their movements to help them improve their condition.

Chapter 2: The Philosophy and Benefits of Tai Chi

Philosophy of Tai Chi

The roots of Tai Chi lie in the Chinese way of life and philosophy, whereas Confucianism and Taoism were the responses to philosophical, social, and political conditions in ancient China. Taoism focused on your mystical and individualistic character and how nature influences this character. Confucianism, on the other hand, is also concerned with human society and social issues.

Millions of people followed the thought patterns defined by Confucius. Most experts are surprised at this since this is one rule many people have followed. Confucius had one goal: to restore order and peace in all provinces. He believed that everybody needed to follow traditional values and follow traditional rules and paths to bring order and peace to their province. He also believed that people understood hierarchy and the order of earth and heaven.

The principles of Taoism lie in the idea that Tao (or the Way) is the reason why everything that is material in the world changes. This is the universal fundamental principle of any change that happens in the world.

You can translate the Tao Te Ching into the Law of Virtue and the path you need to take to abide by it. It became easier for people to put the philosophy of Tao into action when they began to perform and understand Tai Chi. According to Lao Tzu, you should never put yourself against the way things should be. It is important never to try to force the flow of events to change. When you act naturally and let things happen the way they should, you find harmony in your essence. This essence is called the Tao. The idea of the Tao is that the One was born from it. An example of the philosophy of Tai Chi is the story of the Tai Chi master, the emperor, and the bird.

The forces of both the yin and yang came into being when the one created the two. These forces of nature are the opposite of each other. They were also locked in a struggle that is extremely difficult for either of them to win. When one of these forces reached the top, the other found a way to move to the top as well. If you want to live in harmony with Tao, you need to live according to these forces of nature. You also need to maintain an approach in life that is non-interfering.

Maleness represents yang — the light, heat, sun, day, and heaven. On the other hand, yin represents femininity, such as darkness, cold, night, and the moon. All phenomena have these opposite states in them, and these states are termed as the presence in the absence.

Tai Chi uses the principles of Confucianism and Taoism. When you practice Tai Chi, it offers you an outlet for both. China cares about personal defense. The elements of self-improvement and physical action can help you strengthen your mind and body. Most instructors show their students how they should use Tai Chi to resolve the tension in their bodies. They also show their students how to perform inward reflex and outward actions. These movements are central to maintain balance in your body. Here are a couple of points to remember:

- Everything you do and any activity you perform is always a part of the whole

- Any activity you perform includes chi, yin, and yang

- Change is the only constant thing in your life

- Do not force your body into moving; let the movements occur naturally

- Your yin and yang will constantly change

- Be gentle with your body if you want to be strong

Benefits of Tai Chi

Now that you know the Tai Chi philosophy, it is worth looking at some of the benefits.

Reduces Stress

While there is only anecdotal evidence available to confirm that Tai Chi reduces stress, people choose to learn Tai Chi to reduce anxiety. In a study conducted by Zheng et al. (2018), the researchers compared the effects of traditional exercise and Tai Chi on stress. The study was conducted on fifty subjects, and it was noted that Tai Chi and traditional exercise provided the same benefits to help people manage anxiety.

Since Tai Chi also uses focused breathing techniques and meditation, the researchers noted that Tai Chi is more effective than traditional forms of exercise to reduce stress. However, more research is needed to corroborate this.

Unlike some forms of traditional exercise, Tai Chi has a lower impact on the muscles and joints. It is also accessible and easy to perform. Researchers found that Tai Chi is inexpensive and safe. If you experience stress-related anxiety and are healthy, it may be a good idea to choose Tai Chi.

Improves Your Mood

Tai Chi can improve your mood if you are anxious or depressed. A study conducted by Yeung et al. (2017) concluded that Tai Chi, if practiced regularly, could reduce the symptoms of depression and anxiety. Experts believe that mindful, slow movements and breaths affect the central nervous system positively. These activities also regulate mood hormones. Research is being conducted to determine the link between improved mood and Tai Chi.

Better Sleep Cycle

If you want to improve your sleep cycle, you should practice Tai Chi regularly. A study was conducted by Caldwell et al. (2016) for ten weeks on young adults with depression and anxiety. The researchers found that the subjects who practiced Tai Chi regularly found their sleep had improved compared to those who did not. The subjects who practiced Tai Chi also experienced fewer anxiety and depression symptoms. A study conducted by Chan et al. in 2016 showed that older adults could also use Tai Chi to improve their sleep. Researchers found that adults who practiced Tai Chi twice a week for two months slept better than those who did not practice it.

Aids in Weight Loss

If you practice Tai Chi regularly, it can help with weight loss. A study was conducted by Hui, S. et al (2015) to determine how Tai Chi reduces weight. The subjects in the study were older people who practiced Tai Chi for forty-five minutes, five times a week. The researchers noted the weight of the subjects regularly and tracked it for twelve weeks. At the end of the study, they noted that the adults lost over a pound without any changes to their lifestyle.

Improves Cognition

Research shows that Tai Chi can improve cognition, especially in those who have shown signs of cognitive impairment. Tai Chi also increases the ease with which a person can perform any activities. It can also help to improve a person's memory and ability to carry out complex tasks.

Reduces the Risk of Falling

When you do Tai Chi, you need to perform movements that require you to maintain balance. A study conducted by Mortazavi et al. (2018) showed that older adults who perform Tai Chi are not afraid of falling because they know they can control their bodies. Tai Chi also helps to reduce actual falls after a few weeks of practicing Tai Chi. When you are afraid of falling, it reduces the quality of your life and independence. These falls can lead to complications. Studies also showed that Tai Chi improves your wellbeing and quality of life.

Reduces the Symptoms of Fibromyalgia

Experts state that performing Tai Chi helps you to manage and reduce the symptoms of chronic disease. Tai Chi also compliments some traditional pain management methods. A study conducted by Wang et al. (2018) showed that Tai Chi helped reduce several fibromyalgia symptoms. The subjects were asked to participate in Tai Chi for a year. At the end of the study, the researchers noted that participants showed fewer fibromyalgia symptoms than other participants.

Improves Chronic Obstructive Pulmonary Disease (COPD) Symptoms

Research shows that Tai Chi helps to reduce the symptoms of COPD. A study conducted by Wu et al. (2014) on subjects with COPD showed that these subjects could perform exercise easily. These subjects also reported that their lives had improved since they began Tai Chi.

Reduces the Symptoms of Parkinson's Disease

A controlled and randomized trial performed by Li et al. (2012) on 195 subjects showed that Tai Chi helped to reduce the symptoms of Parkinson's disease. People with Parkinson's may regain their balance and become stronger. During the trial, the researchers found that people with the disease did not fall as often as those who did not practice Tai Chi. The art also helps you increase overall balance and leg strength.

It's Safe for People with Heart Disease

If you have heart disease, it is best to perform Tai Chi since it is a light or moderate exercise. If you do have cardiovascular disease, you should practice Tai Chi for the following reasons:

- It makes you physically active
- It becomes easy to lose weight
- It improves the quality of your life

Reduces Pain from Arthritis

A small-scale trial was conducted by Uhlig et al. (2010) with only fifteen subjects. These subjects had rheumatoid arthritis and practiced the art for twelve weeks. The researchers checked in with the subjects at regular intervals and noted that the subjects reported improved balance and mobility and less pain.

Another study was conducted by Wang et al. (2009) on a large scale with forty subjects. These subjects had knee osteoarthritis. They practiced Tai Chi twice a week for twelve weeks. Each session lasted for 60 minutes. At the end of the study, the researchers noted that the subjects showed improved quality of life and mobility. They also found that the subjects reported less pain.

Experts recommend performing Tai Chi instead of undergoing physical therapy since the former is more effective when treating knee osteoarthritis. You must ensure that you speak to your doctor before you begin with Tai Chi. Your doctor can give you a modified version of the movements.

Is it Safe to Practice Tai Chi?

Tai Chi does not have too many side effects since it is considered a safe exercise. If you are a beginner, you may experience aches or pains when you practice it for the first time. Rigorous and difficult forms of Tai Chi can lead to injury. If you do not practice Tai Chi carefully, it may lead to injuries. It is best to find an instructor or join a class if you are new to Tai Chi and want to reduce the potential of any injury. Do not perform Tai Chi if you are pregnant. If you have been performing Tai Chi while pregnant, you need to speak to your doctor to see if it is safe to continue.

Tai Chi focuses on exact movements and posture. It is difficult to learn these on your own, so it is best to take a class or work with an instructor if you are new to Tai Chi. This art is taught all over the United States and other countries. It is best to find something close to your home.

Difference Between Yoga and Tai Chi

Tai Chi is an art that uses fluid movements. As mentioned earlier, this art originated in China, while yoga originated in India, and it focuses on poses and maintaining your breath. Both yoga and Tai Chi are exercise forms that involve deep breathing and meditation and have the following benefits:

- Improves sleep
- Relieves stress
- Improves mood

Dantians

In this section, you will look at the dantians or the energy centers in your body. There are three dantians in the body, and you use each of them when performing Tai Chi. These energy centers in the body control and store both the energy potential and energy in the body. These centers are also termed the three treasures.

Locations of the Dantians

Now, look at where each of these is in the body.

Lower Dantian

The lower dantian, also known as the jing, is found two or three inches below the belly button. This is the source of all energy that will build in the physical body. It allows you to develop the energy and use your shen and qi.

Middle Dantian

The middle dantian, also called qi, is found in the heart. This energy is created from air and food. It is closely related to your thoughts and emotions.

Upper Dantian

The upper dantian or shen is found at the center between your eyebrows. It can be a little higher and is closely related to your consciousness and spirit.

Concerning dantians in Tai Chi, this book will often refer to the lower dantian. Only when a distinction is made are the other dantians considered. A few reasons for considering only the lower dantian are:

> • This is the original and first source of energy or chi in the body

- You cannot feel the other Tai Chi energy points or dantians in the body until there is enough energy in your body. The energy from the lower dantian travels to these parts of the body and lends them some feeling or sensation
- This dantian is the center of all your power

Points to Remember About Dantians

The goal in performing any Tai Chi or Qigong movements is to build the body's energy and increase the circulation of different body fluids, including blood, within the body. You can increase your energy in the dantians easily. You can increase the energy in the dantians and clean the energy if you maintain good posture and breathe freely. The following are a few ways you can increase the energy:

- Maintain good posture
- Improve breathing
- Move the energy from the dantians to other parts of the body
- Coordinate the movements you make with your breath

Relationship Between Dantians and Tai Chi

Tai Chi is an art developed and created very smartly. Every movement you make in Tai Chi is carefully designed. The movements help you build and activate the different energy centers in your body. The creators of Tai Chi developed these movements based on thousands of years of research and refinement. If you are a beginner, you will reap the benefits of Tai Chi from the knowledge learned from your teacher. When you perform any movement in Tai Chi, you learn to let the energy flow through the dantians to the rest of your body. You will look at the importance of the lower dantian in Tai Chi breathing and explain how you need to use it to improve your movements.

Chapter 3: The Five Styles: Chen, Yang, Wu, Sun, and Hao

This chapter will provide you with information on the different styles of Tai Chi. You will also learn how you can choose the right style for you.

The Styles

Chen Style

In the year 1670, a descendant of the Chen family, Chen Wangting, developed different Tai Chi routines based on the classical Chen style of Tai Chi. This form is practiced today by many people across China and other parts of the world. Wangting was influenced by different schools of other arts, such as boxing. Qi Jiguang, a member of the Imperial Army, also influenced him. Wangting used the book written by Jiguang. Wangting also assimilated various techniques of Tuna and Daoyin into his routines. When combined with the use of consciousness and clarity, these techniques led to the development and practice of Taoism.

Tuna and Daovin are very different from each other. The former focuses on breathing and calming exercises, while the latter focuses on exerting inner forces. Several Tai Chi styles also use Qigong exercises that developed from Tuna. Wangting also used aspects of traditional Chinese medicine (TCM). When he combined these styles, the Tai Chi developed by him became a system of exercises that focused on different actions, mental concentration, and breathing. These forms are closely connected. This led to the development of a new style of Tai Chi, which improved all forms of health. When Wangting developed this style of Tai Chi, he did not let any other parts of China know about this style. The clan was very close-knit, and they never taught anybody who would leave the village this style. They did not teach their daughters but taught their daughters-in-law this style of Tai Chi since the former would leave the village.

Another member of the Chen family, Chen Xin, illustrated the art and wrote a book about the Chen style of Tai Chi in his later years. In his book, he talked about the proper movements and postures that one must maintain when they practice Tai Chi. He also explained the medical and philosophical background of every movement and routine. This book was only published in China in 1932. Chen Changxing's grandson, Chen Fake, popularized the Chen style of Tai Chi when he taught people in the Chen village.

Chen Fake was from the Chen family, and he was from the seventeenth generation. He was probably the greatest leader and the most accomplished member of the Chen family. There are numerous stories told in China about his prowess and knowledge in Tai Chi. He was well liked by everybody and made no enemies for as long as he lived in Beijing. He was well known for his perfect disposition.

Chen Fake was the youngest member of the Chen family and was born when his father was around 65 years old. Since Fake's brothers had died because of an epidemic, everybody around him spoiled him, and no one forced him to do the things that he should have done. He was a weakling since he refused to practice Tai Chi. Chen Fake knew his health would improve if he practiced Tai Chi, but he was lazy. He never bothered to practice it, and he soon became a laughingstock in his village. His father was well known for his skill in Tai Chi.

When Fake grew older, he felt ashamed of himself. He did not like how people talked about him and always felt he was letting his father and family down. His cousin was known for his skills. Fake decided to catch up to his cousin and beat him in the art. Since his cousin practiced every day, he continued to improve. Fake practiced every day, but he could not perform the art as well as his cousin. Fake's cousin was strong and an expert in Tai Chi, so Fake began to worry that he could never be as good as his cousin.

One day Chen Fake and his cousin were walking back from their practice in the fields. On their way back, his cousin remembered that he had left something back in the field. He mentioned to Fake that he should run back and bring the item. He also told Fake he would walk slowly so that Fake could catch up with him on his return. When Fake ran toward his cousin, he suddenly realized that he could beat his cousin if he practiced hard. After this realization, he began to practice harder every day. He improved in strength and technique, and he eventually beat his cousin. Since Fake's father was away from home for about three years, nobody could attribute his improvement to his training. Fake's improvement was a direct result of the time he spent practicing every movement and flow.

During his years in Beijing, Chen Fake met and taught thousands of students. Most of his students performed this style of Tai Chi to cure a specific illness or improve their health. A few of Chen's famous students include Li Zhongyiun, Hong Junsheng, Li Jinwu, Tang Hao, Lei Mumin, Feng Zhiqiang, Gu Liuxin, Liu Rui Zhang, and Tian Xiuchen. This style of Tai Chi is characterized using spiritual forces. The movements in this style are like other forms of martial arts. It is a mix of fast and hard movements along with soft and slow movements. The style has a mix of low and powerful stances. The Chen style of Tai Chi is used in combat. The movements are effective and practical, which makes them suitable for the young.

Yang Style

This is the most popular form or style of Tai Chi. Yang Lu-Chan created it during the period 1799 to 1872. Yang had always loved martial arts, and he studied different forms of these arts since he was a child. He also studied with different masters. He used to spar with people from different villages and lost once to a descendent or member of the Chen village. He was impressed by the opponent's form and movements. He had never come across someone who used soft, powerful, and curve-like movements while performing martial arts. He had always learned the hard styles of martial arts.

Yang wanted to learn this soft art. He was quite desperate, so he pretended to faint outside his opponent's house. He acted like a beggar. Yang started to wake up every night and peep into the room where the villagers practiced this art. He mirrored the movements performed by the villagers and soon became a skilled practitioner. When the Chen elders caught Yang, they could have had him executed for his behavior. But the elders were impressed with his skill and took him in as a student.

Yang then left the village and traveled around China to spread awareness of the art. Since there was nobody who could defeat him, he was termed "Yang the invincible." He soon developed his style and taught people he met that same style. He also taught many members of the Imperial Court. This style of Tai Chi is characterized by slow, graceful, and gentle movements. It is easy for anybody to perform these movements. This style also promotes health, and this has become popular these days.

Hao or Wu Style

It is important to note that this Wu style is different from the Wu style discussed in the next section. Many words in Mandarin sound the same but have different meanings. These words are called Pinyins. This style of Tai Chi is also known as Hao. This style was first created by Wu Yuxiang between the years 1812 and 1880. He then passed on this style to Hao Weizheng, who developed the style and added his flair to it between 1849 and 1920. This style is not practiced commonly, and the people who created it studied the Chen and Yang styles of Tai Chi.

Hao is a style of Tai Chi that is characterized by internally slow and loose movements. These movements are close-knit when it comes to the outward experience. In this style of Tai Chi, you need to maintain the right position. The internal power in your body controls any external movement you make. When you look at the higher levels of this style, it will appear more rounded and larger.

Wu Style

The Wu style of Tai Chi was developed between the period 1834 and 1942. It was first introduced by Wu Quan-you and later by his son Wu Jian-Quan. This form of Tai Chi emphasizes the incoming force and the softness placed on the movements. This style is rich in movements and focuses on hand movements and techniques. This style requires you to maintain a leaning posture. This is a pleasant style of Tai Chi and has depth.

Sun Style

The Sun style is the youngest form of Tai Chi and is quite recent. It was created between the period 1861 and 1932 by Sun Lu-tang. Before he learned the art of Tai Chi, he learned two other forms of internal styles of martial arts known as Baguaguan and Xingyiguan. In the year 1912, Sun ran into the creator of the Hao style of Tai Chi. Hao was sick at the time, and Sun took care of Hao. He did not know who Hao was and did his best to find him the right doctor and a hotel for him to stay at. When Hao recovered, he taught Sun Tai Chi.

Sun created his version of Tai Chi based on the Hao style, but he made sure the movements were based on agile steps. When one foot moved either forward or backward, the other foot would also need to move in the same direction. The movements are like a river, and they flow smoothly. There is a powerful exercise that you need to perform every time you change directions. The Sun style of Tai Chi has higher stances.

The exercise performed in the Sun style of Tai Chi is known as Qigong and improves your internal strength. This power is effective when it comes to relaxing and healing. Since the style uses higher stances, it is extremely easy for older people to perform. The style is also compact, which means you do not require a large space to perform the movements. The Sun style of Tai Chi has a lot of depth, and it will hold your interest if you choose to learn it.

How to Choose the Best Tai Chi Style

As discussed earlier, there are five styles of Tai Chi. You can modify and improve the style to suit your fitness levels and goals. All Tai Chi styles ensure you move from one movement to the next easily. The following are a few points to keep in mind when you choose the right style for you:

- The yang chi style focuses on graceful and slow movements. Every move you make will relax you, which is a great point to start with if you are a beginner.

- The Wu style is practiced extremely slowly, and it emphasizes the smaller movements you make.

- The Chen style uses both fast and slow movements, and it may be difficult for you to perform this style of Tai Chi if you are very new to this art.

- The Sun style is like the Chen style, but unlike the Chen style, the Sun style involves less punching, crouching, and kicking. This means it does not demand much from your body.

- The Hao style is not practiced by many people since it is not commonly known. This style focuses more on your internal strength and the accurate positioning of the limbs.

The Style for Beginners

If you find one style more comfortable or can perform the movements easily, you will likely learn to finish it. You will also remember the order movements and can practice the style with ease. You will need to follow the steps below when you want to choose a style:

- It is easy to learn the Wu, Hao, and Yang styles since the physical coordination needed to perform these skills is easy. These styles are easier than the Chen style.

- If your body is tight and you have trouble stretching, you need to stick to the larger Tai Chi styles. It is only through these styles that you can perform the movements easily over time. Your muscles will loosen over time even if you perform the smaller styles of Tai Chi.

- If you have injured knees or a bad lower back, do not perform Tai Chi styles with lower stances since these strain your back. Use smaller styles of Tai Chi if you want a higher stance.

- Large Tai Chi styles improve your leg strength since they have deeper and longer stances.

- The smaller Tai Chi styles are easy since you can easily perform the style's internal work. This is the easiest way to work with the internal organs.

The Style for People Over Fifty

Since the short-form and slow-motion styles of Tai Chi are the easiest to learn, it is best for people over fifty to practice these styles. If you are over fifty and want to learn a long form, it is best to start with a short form since this will help loosen your muscles. You will learn the art easily and absorb, remember, and enjoy the Tai Chi style you have chosen. Styles of Tai Chi that include longer and deeper stances can affect your back and knees. If you are strong, you can take longer and deeper stances at the usual speed. Small styles of Tai Chi, such as Wu, are often the best choice to improve the health of your organs. For people over fifty, it is difficult to make large movements.

Chapter 4: Tai Chi vs. Qigong (Chi Kung)

Introduction to Qigong

Qigong literally translates to work using energy. This is an old form of yoga developed in Asia. It has been around for many years, and this exercise is performed using standing movements. You can also perform this exercise by sitting down. There are different Qigong systems, which you can use to improve the way you work with your breath. These Qigong forms have come from different parts of the world, and each form focuses on one aspect. Most of these forms focus on health, while others focus on martial arts.

The systems in your body work on harnessing this power to help you learn to channel your energy through your palms. Most health practitioners in ancient times used to channel this energy to heal their patients. You can do this easily if you learn to focus better on the systems. Some different monasteries and temples focus on the depth and spiritual cultivation of medication. Some forms involve the use of movements, while others are based on visualization. All these forms use specialized breathing while you continue to perform the activity on hand. The principle that guides these practices focuses on coordinating the body's movements and eyes, your breath, the focus of your mind, and more. If you want to perform non-movement and passive exercises, you need to focus on your inward vision. You also learn to explore different inner realms when you let your breath guide you.

Now this book will take the time to explain this formula better. It will dissect it so that you can understand each detail. The objective of Qigong is to coordinate between these aspects. Consider the following if you want Qigong to be effective.

Eyes in Qigong

When it comes to Western civilization, the eyes are termed as the gateway to your soul. According to Taoism, the eyes are used to guide the spirit or the shen. It is believed that the energy in the body follows the spirit while the body fluids, including blood, will follow the qi.

The eyes in your body work as the command center. You can use your eyes to manage the energy in the body. Your eyes also help you control the flow of energy in the body. When you master this, you can learn to project the energy outward and influence your environment.

Body Movements in Qigong

The body movements in Qigong follow a sequence, and each sequence has a different set of exercises. Every exercise in the sequence uses the different energy meridians or pathways that are present in your body. Through these exercises, you learn to trace the edges in the energy fields in your body. You also learn to embrace and smoothen the body's energy fields to help you manage the potency of the flow of energy through your body. These movements involve the use of different degrees of energy and exertion. The exercises can be rigorous if you are a beginner.

If you want to learn more about how this works, read the story of the Shaolin temple and Bodhidharma. Bodhi created a routine known as the Eighteen Hands of Lohan. When this routine is mixed with Kung Fu, you may exert yourself. This form of martial arts is more like yoga. You can hold static postures or emphasize the flow of energy and the continuity of motion.

Mental Focus in Qigong

This is an important aspect of Qigong and its practice. Most students overlook this art of breathing. If you want to master Qigong, you need to pay close attention to every critical energy component in your body. Qigong also engages in the energy stored in the heart. This energy is mapped to the fire element. The energy in the heart works with the spirit. Experts believe that the link between intention and attention will help you master life. In Qigong, you need to focus on different body movements and learn to track them with your eyes. To do this, you need to focus your mind and learn to be in the present. The reward of this process is immense. You also learn to draw on the energy from the earth.

Use of Breath in Qigong

Your breath circulates in your body through different meridians. This is the energy from the air, and it combines with the qi from the food you consume to produce energy in your body. It is the coordination between attention and body movements that open blockages and free the pathways. In Qigong, you learn to use your breath to gather and store it as energy in different reservoirs, known as dantians, in your body. You also learn to push the energy through different pathways in your body. If you are a beginner, you need to make an effort to learn how to extract energy from the air through your breath.

This may seem simple, but this framework will set a precedent for the energy and magic you use in Qigong. There is a lot of information you need to learn about the different movements in

Qigong. Learning as much as you can is the only way to learn everything there is to know about your body's energy paths and how the energy affects you. Even if you do not understand the mechanics but learn everything about the coordinated thoughts, movements, and breathing, you will be ahead of your game.

The subject of these pathways is very new to people, and you will learn more about them in this chapter. You will look at the different mechanisms of action and understand them better. You will also learn about your intellect and how you can engage it through intention and attention. When you activate the vertical axis of your soul, you activate the energies of fire, water, and earth. You will finally unlock the first hints of the potential in your body. It is only when you do this that you can make powerful changes in your body.

The vertical axis in your body will give you the necessary spiritual and mental alignment to help you connect easily with your body. You need to do this while you practice Qigong. When you connect different aspects of yourself through the practice of Qigong, you learn to snap out of the area of wants and needs. When you learn to divert your body's energy from the harmful and wasteful patterns, you learn to connect with the energy. You also learn to accumulate and gather the power in your reservoir and use this energy as a buffer to help you overcome fatigue, disease, and lack of energy. When I say storing or accumulating energy and power, you need to create places to condense and refine the energy quality that flows through you. You can condense the energy to nourish your being and refine it, so it helps to illuminate your spirit.

You need to be extremely careful when it comes to your views on this aspect. Do not look at it in terms of capitalism—since this changes your understanding of the art. Your outlook on the energy in your body changes how you approach life. You never require too much energy in your body since there is always enough energy present in the universe. All the energy in the body and who you will be is in the present moment and is changeable.

It is extremely important for you to learn how to acquire energy from the universe. Before you acquire energy, you need to learn where this energy comes from. You cannot draw the energy from an outside source, like a river or well. The force of the universe and the energy is flowing through you every minute. It flows through every organ in your body, and the blocks you create in your being that lead to the sense of lacking since the energy stops flowing easily through your body. When you channel this imbalanced energy through your body and into your shadows, you close off your mind. You let it limit your energy and change the definition of who you are. You are also exhausted.

The Objective of Qigong

When it comes to Qigong, you do not focus on adding anything to your body. It is mostly about the removal of negative energy. When you learn to get more out of your practice, you learn to let the universal energy flow into your body. You learn to use the energy from the universe and become an agent of its will. It is only when you do this that you take your rightful place. By rightful place, this does not mean you will need to focus on far-off achievements; you will learn to live in the present.

Through Qigong, you learn to wake up and live in the current moment. You learn to take part in the present. This is an important aspect to consider when you want to eliminate any unwanted energies in your body. You remove the frustration, grief, and anger in your horizontal axis. Your horizontal soul is closely related to the falling and rising trends of your emotional and mental upheavals. This upheaval is closely tied to your life. Learn to focus on this process and focus on balancing these axes.

People often find themselves stuck at this stage since they repress most of their emotions and needs in their shadows. Most people suffer and cling to things that do not matter because of the energy they get from wood and metal. The former energy is your desire for more, while the latter is the energy to let go of things. Most people continue to hold on to negativity, and the energy in the body is imbalanced. This imbalance leads to the creation of monsters in the body.

According to traditional Chinese medicine, the lungs are important since they represent the metal element. The energy from these elements moves naturally. The liver represents energy from wood, which is naturally found. The lungs are above the liver in the body, and the essence of life is dependent on the maintenance and management of the dynamic tension and flow of energy. The body needs to maintain the inverted forces of energy. The energy from the lungs is pushed down, while the energy from the liver is pushed upward. When you die, the energy from the liver moves to heaven while the energy from the lungs moves into the earth. It is important to check the dynamic tension between these forms of energy. If you do not manage it, the energy will separate and perish.

People's lives run smoother when they learn to maintain the flow of energy in the body. You need to harmonize the flow of the energy on the horizontal axis since this helps you plug into the power of the energy on the vertical axis. The alignment of intention and attention is something you need to understand. It is only when you understand this that you can understand your condition. Do not run away from your innermost thoughts and emotions. You need to be more aware, engaged, and live in the moment.

Differences

Now that you know what Qigong is look at a few differences between Tai Chi and Qigong.

Tai Chi is One Form of Qigong

Qigong forms the basics of Tai Chi. You focus on your mind and breath in Qigong and do the same in Tai Chi. You can only maintain this focus when you master the art of Qigong.

Qigong focuses on healing and wellness, while Tai Chi is a martial art.

Qigong uses different exercises for healing. Tai Chi, on the other hand, does not focus on healing. Many people practice different forms of Tai Chi for healing and wellbeing. Qigong does not focus on any attack, fighting, or defense movements like Tai Chi does. The various Qigong movements can improve your self-defense techniques and power, especially if you practice Kung Fu or Tai Chi.

Different Movements

Qigong does not use many standing movements. You can perform Qigong while lying or sitting down. Tai Chi focuses on standing movements. Both Tai Chi and Qigong focus on careful and slow movements in general.

They Use Qi Differently

There are different exercises in Qigong, which focus or use Qi differently. This is especially true when it comes to medical Qigong. In Tai Chi, the movements do not do this. The movements in Tai Chi use whole-body movements and functions. Each of these movements uses qi differently.

The Difference in Complexity of Movement

From the previous section, you know the movements used in Qigong are simple. Tai Chi, on the other hand, uses many complex stances and movements.

Qigong Does Not Have Forms

From the previous chapter, you know there are different forms of Tai Chi. Qigong, on the other hand, only uses one form. It is only based on a series of structures of exercises. You can tailor these exercises based on your health. You can also perform these exercises whenever you want to.

Qigong is Easier than Tai Chi

A few stances and movements in Tai Chi are difficult to perform. If you have any injury or physical restriction, it may be easier for you to perform Qigong. Since Qigong uses free movements, it is easier for you to adapt to this form of martial arts. You can modify the movements in Qigong to suit your abilities and needs.

Chapter 5: Tai Chi Meditation and Breathwork

If you are a beginner, you may find the idea of sitting quietly in a room a little strange. It is hard to sit with your innermost feelings and thoughts. You may find it hard to sit and do absolutely nothing. Your mind will completely resist this. Meditation can feel alien to you if you are a beginner. It may also feel daunting, but this is fine. Meditation is a practice people have followed for over 3,000 years.

You may want to start meditating for different reasons. You probably want to feel less stressed, focus more, or be less reactive. Meditation may also be a part of personal development. You can choose to meditate to improve your relationship with the people around you. Regardless of what the reason is, you need to train your mind to become more aware. This is one of the easiest ways for you to change your perception of life.

You experience everything through your mind. Your perception of life may change dramatically when you begin to meditate. You may be inspired to meditate, but thinking about meditating is different from doing it. You will only reap the benefits of meditation when you begin practicing it. It is important to develop a regular practice, too. Before you meditate, make sure your mind is calm.

Learn to understand its untamed behavior. Meditation is extremely simple; however, you need to keep a few points in mind before you start.

Learning the Experience

If you are a beginner, it is best to use guided meditation techniques. You can either perform the activity with an instructor or use a recording. Do not expect your mind to remain calm. It will be restless, easily distracted, and busy. Yes, you have chosen to meditate and focus on your mind. This does not mean you will suddenly experience a calm mind. You cannot expect to train your dog overnight.

As mentioned earlier, meditation is an easy and straightforward process. You only need to practice it regularly. The only thing you need to do is close your eyes and focus on your breathing. Allow your mind to do what it wants. Meditation is the only skill where you do not have to achieve an objective. This activity is only a place where you do not have to put any effort.

Meditation is not good or bad. You are either aware or unaware. When you find yourself lost in thought and learn to reel yourself in, you become aware. This is when you learn to return to your object of focus—that is, your breath. You need to keep doing this if you want to return to your meditation process. Your objective should be to hone your awareness. When you persevere and meditate regularly, the period between your distraction and awareness will grow longer.

Before you start, you need to familiarize yourself with how your mind functions and works. You need to know what to expect when you begin to meditate. It is important to note that meditation does not solve any of your problems. You cannot expect a life filled with happiness simply because you meditate. Life will continue to happen, and it will throw different situations and uncertainties at you. Meditation helps you choose how you react to different situations. You will change the way you react. You also learn how to view a circumstance differently. When you practice consistently, you can change the way you feel about any situation. You become more aware and understand different aspects of life better.

The Practicalities

Before you look at how meditation helps in Tai Chi, you will first learn about the different practicalities you need to remember.

Find the Right Place and Time

The objective is to commit to meditating regularly. You need to meditate at least a few times each week if possible. You must be clear about how much time you want to spend on meditation. You also need to determine where you want to sit. Since this is a habit you need to develop, it will take perseverance and discipline. It is only when you honor the routine that you can build on your practice. Most people meditate around the same time, just like they perform a routine habit, such as brushing their teeth or eating breakfast. This is the only way they can remember to meditate. It is best to meditate every morning. Alternatively, you can find a time that works for you.

Clothing

You can wear anything you want. The objective of meditation is to help you remain relaxed and comfortable. If you are wearing a belt, scarf, or tie, remove them before you sit down to meditate. Remove any uncomfortable clothing or tight shoes. You can also sit without any clothing in the comfort of your home if this helps you.

Position

Where you meditate and how you sit does not matter. You can either meditate outside or inside. You can choose to sit on a cushion, the floor, chair, bench, or any other place that works best for you. You can choose to sit in a cross-legged position under a tree if you want to follow the stereotypical images. If you are a beginner, you can sit in an upright position on a chair or the floor. You need to familiarize yourself with the practice. It is best to sit toward the front of the chair since that helps you keep your neck relaxed, your back straight, and your chin tucked in. Leave your hands on your lap.

Time

The time you spend meditating depends on your circumstances, the time available, and your preference. It is important to note that the time you spend on meditation is not as important as how often you meditate. When you begin with meditation, it is best to start with a short session. You can increase the time slowly until you become familiar with training your mind. If you cannot sit in silence for a long time, you can choose a three-minute session. Give meditation a shot and learn to improve your skills as your confidence grows.

Define Your Motivation

People meditate for different reasons, and for this reason, nobody can define the reasons. It is always helpful for you to start with a clear idea about why you want to meditate. If you do not have a clear motivation in mind, you cannot meditate. You will struggle to maintain this habit. When you are clear about your motivation, you know exactly what you want from the session. You may choose to meditate to be more focused, feel calmer, and be less stressed or be happier. This motivation will help you maintain the right attitude. You also learn to commit and maintain the practice of meditation.

Take Each Day as it Comes

Bear in mind that meditation is a practice. You cannot expect to sprint and learn everything in one session. You cannot expect instant progress. Take every session as it comes. You need to appreciate the skill and commit to it. Be patient and practice regularly. You will feel the benefits of this practice over time. Meditation is neither good nor bad, and you cannot succeed or fail. Meditation only focuses on non-awareness and awareness. Through meditation, you learn to let go of distractions. The more your mind learns about your thoughts and emotions, the more you learn to become aware. You learn to eliminate distractions.

Learn to Stay Mindful After Meditation

When you meditate, you learn to practice being in the present moment. You learn to be more aware of what is happening now. The objective of meditation is to remove any distractions during the day and become more mindful of your thoughts. When you finish your session, take time to recognize how your thoughts have changed. You need to intend to carry on this feeling throughout your day. You also need to develop a clear idea of what you will do immediately after your meditation session. This can be any activity. You can jump off the seat and become active straight away. Try not to let go of the spacious quality you developed during the meditation session, so be more aware of this quality regardless of the type of activity you perform.

Use Body Scans

One of the best ways to begin with meditation if you are a beginner is through a body scan. This technique is one of the easiest ways to cultivate the curiosity you need to bring to meditation. So, what is a body scan? Consider a photocopier or X-ray machine. This machine is slowly moving on every part of your body. It detects the different physical sensations in your body and any changes you may make in your body. This machine does not analyze any of your thoughts or change the way you feel.

This book will now explain the technique a little better. You close your eyes and start focusing on the top of your head. You need to scan your body from your head to your toes mentally. As you perform this scan, notice the parts of your body that are tensed and those that are relaxed. Identify the parts of your body that are uncomfortable or comfortable. The only thing you are doing is developing a picture of how your body feels. Take twenty seconds to complete this process. You may find yourself distracted and different thoughts may arise. If you are distracted, go back to the part of your body where you left off. When you make this technique a part of your practice, you become familiar with your feelings and emotions.

Obstacles Beginners Often Face

If you are a beginner and meditating for the first time, you will encounter a few obstacles. You may be bored, anxious, overwhelmed, generally resistant, restless, or worried. When you continue to meditate, you learn to overcome these obstacles. The process becomes easier. It is important to remember that you approach meditation only with a lifetime of being conditioned. Your mind is always busy, and it cannot work with stillness. So, your mind will not work in your favor until it adjusts to the idea of not doing anything and letting things go.

Finding the Time

Most people face a common obstacle when it comes to meditation: They cannot find the time to meditate. It is important to note that you can miss meditation for a few days a week. It is important to practice meditation regularly, but if you can pick up from your last session and learn to give yourself time to meditate, you learn to improve the health of your mind. If you last meditated a week or month ago, revisit the basics because your mind may not remember everything you taught it.

Feeling Drowsy

It is normal for people to fall asleep or feel drowsy when they meditate. If you are a beginner, this can happen frequently. The mind believes that doing nothing means you are relaxing. You will learn to differentiate between total relaxation, which results from meditation, and relaxed focus, which you achieve through meditation. The following are a few tips you can use to remain alert and awake:

- Do not lie down when you meditate. Maintain an upright posture.

- It is best to meditate in the morning when your mind is a little brighter and you are not tired after your day at work or school.

- Let fresh air into the room.

Multiple Distractions

Most beginners believe you need complete silence when you meditate. If you have this thought in mind, any distraction or sound around you will make you extra sensitive. However, you do not have to sit in complete silence when you meditate. You need to settle down in your environment and let the sounds surrounding you become background noise. Children are going to yell in the street, and your neighbors may play loud music. Learn to settle into your background. Do not dwell on the sounds around you. Try to tune the sounds out and avoid getting frustrated. If you are a beginner, you will struggle with this, but you can use noise-canceling earphones or earplugs to help you during your session.

Stereotypes

Meditation is a practice or tradition that comes with numerous stigmas and misconceptions attached to it. Meditation is a practice built on the back of many stereotypes built on the back of various media, rumors, and myths. Most people associate meditation with different images and labels they may have read or seen. Bear in mind that you do not need a "specific" personality to meditate. Anybody can meditate. People who want to understand their minds better can start meditating—so can you.

One of the biggest misconceptions or myths of meditation is that it is a religious practice. You need to understand that meditation does not rely on your belief system, but it is a skill. Some people meditate in certain religions; however, using this skill in religious practices does not make meditating religious.

Another stereotype is that people believe meditation is serious. You need to sit in a cross-legged position, extend your arms, and repeat a sound loudly. The truth is very different. You can choose to sit in a cross-legged position, by the beach, in nature, or even meditate on a chair. The only thing you need to do is become aware of everything that happens in your mind. You need to focus on your feelings and emotions. Since everyone has different thoughts, they struggle differently. Many athletes have begun to use meditation to help them calm their minds. They use this to train their minds to not get in their way when they participate.

People who meditate do not hug trees or burn incense when they meditate. There is nothing wrong with doing either of these things. The only thing people do when they meditate is get inside their minds and start to understand their thinking processes.

Learn to Stick with the Routine

You can start something new easily, whether it is an exercise regime, a hobby, or a diet. The hard part is to continue performing this activity. Your enthusiasm will begin to wane, and the novelty of the new activity will wear off. This is something that happens with meditation, too. Since the exercises are repetitive, you may get bored. It is important to remember that you are training your mind to work the way you relate to your feelings and thoughts. It will take time, discipline, and perseverance to manage your thoughts and emotions.

People stop meditating because their minds will not allow them to find peace. It is also important to note that your mind is constantly going to think. Your mind is programmed to behave this way. Through meditation, you cannot expect your thoughts to stop completely. Meditation only teaches you how to step back and observe each thought carefully without any bias or judgment. The objective of meditation is to let your thoughts pass through your mind freely. This is a skill you need to master, learn, and practice. You can only do this if you learn to build the habit.

It is only when you stick to your practice of meditation that you will reap its benefits. When you feel the benefits, you learn to understand how your mind feels and thinks. You also learn to take a step toward a happier and healthier life with increased contentment, compassion, calm, and clarity.

Several people refer to Tai Chi as moving meditation. Since this martial art uses graceful and slow movements, it can be used as a meditation technique. This technique helps you maintain focus and control your thoughts and emotions. Tai Chi meditation also leaves you with a feeling of relaxation, which helps you release any inner tensions.

Tai Chi and Meditation

Tai Chi focuses on the flow of energy throughout your body. This science is termed neigong. Every Taoist energy or Qigong system in China uses this science as its foundation. Most martial arts use some or all of the information and techniques that derive from this science. Neigong is the root of the work of chi and is used in martial arts, such as Hsing-I, Bagua and Tai Chi, Chinese medicine techniques, and Taoist meditation. This science is also used in bodywork systems. If you want to learn Tai Chi or any other form of these martial arts, you need to start with the basic movements.

For instance, there are long and short Tai Chi forms, and you have looked at these in detail in the third chapter of the book. Bagua, on the other hand, uses a single palm change or circle walking change. The different components of neigong, over time, will allow you to incorporate the movements and manage the energy easily. You can do this by opening different channels of energy in your body, spirit, and mind.

It is important to learn and understand the components that are relevant to practicing and manipulating energy. You may only learn the basics when you start by practicing this art. As you continue to work, you will move on and learn deeper aspects of the art. You can only do this if you are willing to incorporate the movements to understand your thoughts and emotions. You will constantly return to the different neigong components in the art to learn more about the different powerful and refined applications and aspects within these movements.

There are sixteen components you need to learn, and the sequence is not set in stone. Many people find it easier to learn more about the alignment and breathing components before moving on to find a way to relax and heal. If you are a Tai Chi practitioner, you will experience systematic and progressive physical and mental health improvements. You also learn more about the spiritual and energetic capabilities of your spirit, mind, and body. This combination of different techniques is what makes Tai Chi and other martial arts great for spiritual practices.

Finding Emptiness

When it comes to Taoism or Taoist traditions, you need to embark on a spiritual path that goes beyond having a calm, peaceful, and healthy mind. The objective of Taoist meditation is to make sure that you become aware of the unchanging and permanent center of your existence. You need to find the place of emptiness and spirit.

This is your consciousness. Taoist meditation is a way to relax your mind and soul. You need to relax your very being or soul.

Tai Chi is an art that helps you deepen your understanding of your thoughts, awareness, and the ability to relax on every level. The objective of Tai Chi and the practice of the art is an advanced form of Taoist meditation. You explore different opposites and learn the essence of non-duality and emptiness. These concepts are the foundation of Wu Chi and Tai Chi. You can practice these methods by altering the rhythms of the yin and yang. You only need to perform the movements slowly.

The objective of Tai Chi or moving meditation is difficult to recognize. You need to find the place in your mind where you can combine these differentiations and unite with the emptiness in your mind and soul.

Tai Chi Meditation Techniques

Now, look at a few meditation techniques used in Tai Chi.

Standing Meditation

Cynthia McMullen is an LMT from the Oriental Healing Arts of Massage Therapy, Traditional Taoist Medical Qigong, and Acupuncture in Arizona. She states that meditation is extremely important when performing Tai Chi since it centers and grounds you emotionally and physically. You learn to identify stillness and calm within movements. Since Tai Chi uses standing movements, you use standing meditation when you perform any movement. Follow the steps given below if you want to master this form of meditation.

- You need to stand in a comfortable position. Make sure your feet are shoulder-width apart and your toes are pointing ahead. You can keep your knees relaxed if you want to.

- Tuck your hips a little forward and bend your shoulders downward and keep them relaxed.

- Now, lift your head and hold it high. Do not put too much stress on your neck.

- Take a deep breath and exhale slowly through your nostrils. Now, close your eyes and start focusing on each breath you take. You can keep your eyes slightly open if you want to.

- Focus only on your connection to the ground. Pay attention to your feet and how they feel on the surface of the earth.

- When you inhale, visualize that the energy from the surface around you or the earth is the energy being pulled into your feet. When you exhale, release the energy from your body and let it return to the source.

Continue to perform this exercise fifteen times. Let the energy travel from your legs to the rest of your body. The energy should reach the center of your being. The center of your being is at the sacral chakra, which is right below your belly button. When you exhale, visualize that all the unclean and toxic energy from your body is leaving.

Variations

McMullen also mentioned there are variations to the standing technique. Several variations include arms around the shoulders, seated meditation, meditation with the feet wider than shoulder-width apart, etc.

Focus on Breathing

Dr. Paul Lam is from the Tai Chi Association in Australia. He mentioned that breathing techniques are important when it comes to Tai Chi meditation. When you perform Tai Chi, you need to focus on the energy moving between your body and the surrounding area. It is important to note that Tai Chi focuses on the giving and taking of energy. The foundation of this form of meditation is extremely easy. You only need to think of absorbing energy when you inhale and releasing it when you exhale. Most Tai Chi movements and meditations use this technique.

Open and Close Movements

Lam also mentioned that you could use open and closed movements when you want to meditate. When you perform opening movements, you need to place your hands in front of your chest. As you inhale, you need to open your arms, step forward, and open them wide open. When you exhale, move your hands closer together and let go of all the pent-up energy. Lam also mentioned that you could apply the same rules when you move up and down. When you move your hands upward, you need to take a deep breath in. As you exhale, get rid of all the toxic energy and let go. When you stand up and bend down, you should breathe in and exhale, respectively.

Tai Chi and Breathing

You may be overwhelmed with the details and other information about Tai Chi. This is another topic that may overwhelm you if you are a beginner. However, you do not have to worry too much about Tai Chi breathing. The objective should be to learn how to move when you practice Tai Chi. Your breathing will improve when you perform and practice Tai Chi. When you learn the form completely and have practiced for a while, you need to learn how to breathe. You will also learn when to inhale and exhale.

Common postures used in Tai Chi are waving, windmills, and whips. The practice of these movements is more about the placement of the various parts of your body. Your breathing is of utmost importance because your breath is what guides you. Ramel Rones, a Tai Chi master, states, "When practiced regularly, Tai Chi can lead to better health and a higher quality of physical and emotional life." Regardless of whether you perform Tai Chi movements or any other workout, you need to breathe effectively to make sure you meet your fitness goals.

Tai Chi breathing is like the high any runner or athlete will achieve when exercise does not leave them feeling exhausted. This form of breathing will help calm your body down to achieve the balance to perform the exercise in a flow. When you find yourself in this position, you can start working on improving your movements.

If you want to find yourself in that zone, you need to focus on the lower energy center in your body. This center is in the sacral chakra, which is right below your belly button. You need to learn to tap into this area when you perform Tai Chi. This is the only way you can improve your movements and release any stress. Experts recommend that you visualize yourself inhaling and exhaling the energy in this chakra when performing any movement.

Performing Tai Chi Breathing

Follow the steps given below if you want to perform Tai Chi breathing:

- You can either sit or stand in a comfortable position. Let your hand rest on your lap or lower abdomen. If you want to perform Tai Chi breathing, you need to let your tongue rest on the roof of your mouth. You also need to breathe only through your nose. If you want to use Tai Chi breathing when you perform the exercise, it is best to leave this passageway open. You can use both your mouth and nose to breathe when you perform these movements. As you practice, you will learn to breathe only through your nose.

- Take a deep breath and use your diaphragm to push the air into your lungs. Focus on your hands when you inhale. You will see that your hands move upward when you inhale and fall when you exhale.

- You should let your breathing be continuous. When one breath ends, you need to move to the next. Every inhalation and exhalation should form a loop. There should be no end. The objective is to achieve the meditative state where breathing comes naturally to you. Your breathing should be effortless.

- You should now relax your body and let your breath become deeper and longer.

Why You Shouldn't Focus on Tai Chi Breathing

Every movement performed in Tai Chi is scripted. This means the movements are frequently corrected. Most people naturally believe there is breathwork that corresponds to each movement you make. If you focus too much on your breath, you will forget why you want to perform Tai Chi. The objective is only to return and relax the body so you find balance and equilibrium.

It is also hard to define what Tai Chi breathing is all about since different forms of Tai Chi use different breathing patterns. You need to make sure you maintain long continuous breaths. Several movements in Tai Chi also require you to take quick, short breaths. You can employ these breaths when you perform long movements or want to transition quickly from one movement to the next.

When you use standard instructions for breathing when you perform different Tai Chi movements, you do not focus on your current energy state. You also forget about the energy you began with. Assume you enter work or class hyper because you drank too much coffee. When you go back home, perhaps you are exhausted or under the weather because of the work you did. How you start the movements and breaths at the start of any form is different from when you end that form.

The most important thing to remember is that people have different levels of coordination, speed of movements, and lung capacities. If you try to match anybody else, you may only hamper your progress. The subsequent sections will discuss how breathing affects your Tai Chi movements. Different Tai Chi breathing exercises allow you to isolate the breathing from the movement you make.

Now that you have an idea of what Tai Chi breathing is look at a few tips to help you reap the benefits of Tai Chi breathing.

Guidelines for Tai Chi Breathing

Yes, there are no rules for how you should breathe when you perform Tai Chi. This does not mean you can breathe any way you want to. You need to adhere to the following guidelines when you perform Tai Chi:

- When you exhale, breathe out slowly. Exhale for as long as you can. This will leave you feeling like you need to inhale deeply.

- You need to exhale for longer than you inhale.

- Let your tongue stick to the roof of your mouth. If you do not know where to place it, say "la" and see where your tongue is. You need to leave the tongue in this position when you practice Tai Chi.

- Inhale and exhale only through your nose. Do not use your mouth unless you suffer from a cold or an allergy that causes nasal congestion.

- Aim for continuous and long breaths. Do not pause between inhalation and exhalation. Do not stop breathing.

- You must inhale into your belly. When you breathe, the pressure on your organs will change, and each breath massages the organs.

• As you inhale, your body will store energy. So, as you inhale, think of oxygen entering your body. When you deliver this force or energy, you can exhale slowly.

• When you move your hands apart, you need to breathe in deeply. This means you are storing energy.

• If you move your hands up, you need to take a deep breath and store the energy. When you move your hands down, exhale and release the energy into the universe.

Integrating Tai Chi Breathing into Your Workout

According to several classical and ancient Tai Chi texts and documents, you can overcome weight problems with less physical effort using Tai Chi. This suggests that Tai Chi is a better way to complete a workout since it is less stressful on your body. Rones stated, "Through correct postural alignment, deep breathing, an empty mind, and grounding or rooting [connecting with the earth beneath your feet], one can reach a state of effortless action."

The following tips can help you focus on Tai Chi breathing when you perform the movements.

Observe Your Breath

Before you learn to adjust your breathing to follow Tai Chi breathing, you need to become aware of how you currently breathe. You may assume your body only inhales and exhales when you need air, but it will react differently under stress. You may breathe sporadically or in short bursts under stress. When you become mindful about your breath, you can correct any irregularities with ease. You will only need to focus on deep, slow breaths.

Count it Out

If you find yourself unable to breathe, inhale for three seconds and exhale for five seconds. Count every breath you take. The objective is to breathe in a way that feels natural. Do not force your breath. When you gasp for air while you work out, it means you are pushing your limits too hard. Learn to focus on your breathing in such situations. Draw deliberate and deep breaths. Use your diaphragm to take deeper breaths. Check your progress every few minutes to make sure you breathe easily and efficiently. This is the only way you can improve your performance and movements.

Pace Yourself

If you do not want to follow the three- and five-second breaths mentioned in the previous section, you can switch to a shorter duration. You can inhale for one second and exhale for two seconds. You can reduce the speed at which you perform the movements in Tai Chi if you feel tired quickly. If you think it is too fast, take a little more time to breathe in and out. When you perform any strenuous movements, you need to inhale and exhale to make sure your breathing guides your movements. For instance, when you need to bend your knees and move your arms at the same time, inhale when you lower your body and exhale when you move your arms to either side.

Be Self-Aware in Your Routine

It is important to pay attention to what your body is saying to you. You can work out and perform strenuous movements on one day, while you may not have the energy to do this on the next day. So, become aware of how you feel, both physically and mentally. When you practice this, you become more sensitive to what your body has to say. You become more aware, and your performance improves. If you want to do this, you need to ask yourself the following questions when you perform Tai Chi:

- Do I enjoy Tai Chi?
- Is there a way I can enhance the effect the workout has on me?
- Is my breathing too fast?
- Am I connected to my body?

Relax

According to your brain, you need to breathe if you want to live. So, when you stop breathing in, your mind will switch into the fight-or-flight mode. This will lead to panicked and short breaths to make up for the lack of oxygen in your body. If you want to prevent this from happening, you need to slow down and take a few deep breaths. Start observing your breath.

When you practice these steps, your breathing style will improve. If you need an energy booster to go faster, longer, and further, you need to learn how to tap into the energy stored in your body. It is only easy to do this when you maintain your breath.

Why You Shouldn't Pay Too Much Attention to Breathing

If you only focus on your breathing, it can lead to the following consequences:

- If you hold your breath for too long, it can cause anxiety. This will only cause stress, and it defies the purpose of Tai Chi.
- When you relax, the energy from your body moves to your feet or dantian. If you use too much pressure, which you use in Qigong breathing, you may push the energy in the wrong direction.
- You can only feel the energy in your body moving from one organ to the next if you let your breath move freely. You need to learn how to sense your breath and feel it before you manipulate it.

- The worst-case scenario is intestinal problems. If you are under too much pressure, your hemorrhoids can flare up, and you may develop intestinal issues.

The objective of Tai Chi is always to focus on the present and your center. You need to find a balance between your mind, body, and spirit. You can do this easily through Tai Chi breathing. Most people who find themselves in a state, such as being stressed, tired, or agitated, will feel happy and calm after performing Tai Chi breathing. This is something powerful.

Chapter 6: Stances and Footwork

Tai Chi Stances

Before you look at the different training techniques you need to follow in Tai Chi, you will learn about the most important aspect: the fundamental stances. It is only when you perform these stances that you develop a strong foundation of the various postures you need to use when you perform different Tai Chi movements.

You can understand the set of exercises well when you understand these stances. If you are a beginner, you will need to perform these stances and master them if you want to strengthen your muscles. Practice these stances if you want to use your mind to help you practice the different Tai Chi stances. These movements help you coordinate between your movements, breathing, and mind.

When you learn the basics of training, you need to move toward Qigong. Moving Qigong will help you feel the movements the way you need to. The movements will help you maintain and harmonize the energy in your mind, spirit, and body. You can also manage your chi. This book will discuss a few other stances and movements later. Like other martial arts forms, Tai Chi has its fundamental stances, and these are the basics for movement, stability, and martial art techniques. There are eight important stances in Tai Chi, and none of these stances use any hand sequence.

In this chapter, you will look at eight stances. You can ignore the position of your hands when you perform these stances.

Ma Bu or Horse Stance

This stance is often used when you move from one movement to the next. You can use this even when you move from one technique to the next. If you want to perform this stance, you need to perform the steps given below:

- Place your feet wider than shoulder-width apart.
- Bend the knees slowly until the angle between your calves and rear thighs is almost 90 degrees.
- Keep your back straight.
- Relax yourself and center your thoughts and emotions.
- Your knees should be in line with your toes and your feet flat on the ground.

If you want to reduce the stress placed on your body, keep your feet relaxed. This reduces the risk of injury. Your knees should always be in line with your toes when you perform this stance.

Gong JianBu, Deng Shan Bu, Bow-Arrow Stance or Mountain Climbing Stance

This is an important stance since it is an offensive stance used in Tai Chi. To perform this stance, you need to follow the steps given below:

- Place one leg in front of the other. Your toes and knees should be perpendicular to the ground.

- The front leg should support at least 60 percent of your weight.

- The toe of the leg, which is in the lead position, should point toward the inside at a 15-degree angle.

- Set the rear leg firmly on the ground until it supports your body's weight. You can bend the rear leg a little in this stance.

- Maintain the upper body at a 90-degree angle from the ground.

If you make a mistake when it comes to maintaining this stance, you may hurt your knee.

Zuo Pan Bu or Sitting on Crossed Legs Stance

This is a forward movement. You need to first switch to the first stance, the ma bu stance. Once you do this, you need to turn the right foot and body in a clockwise direction. You need to maintain a 90-degree angle between the right foot while you pivot or move on the left foot. You can do the same on your left side. Try to hold the position for at least one minute if you are a beginner. If you have practiced this stance, you can maintain it for at least five minutes.

Si Liu Bu or Four-Six Stance

This stance is used when you try to defend yourself. When it comes to weight distribution, this stance is the opposite of the second stance you looked at. The front leg should support at least forty percent of your weight. Shift the remaining weight onto the back leg. Your rear leg should be slightly bent, and the toes and knees should be turned toward the inside. Hold the front leg slightly loose and bend it. Do not strain any part of your body.

Fu Hu Bu or Tame the Tiger Stance

The tame the tiger stance is used for defense. You can also use this stance when you perform low attacks. Follow the steps given below to assume this stance:

- Stand with your feet shoulder-width apart.

- While keeping one leg straight, lower your body slowly while squatting down on one leg.

- When you squat, your thigh should be parallel to the floor.

- Your feet need to be flat on the ground, while the knee of the squatting leg is in line with your toes.

Xu Bu, Xuan Ji Bu or False Stance

The false stance helps to strengthen your body to increase the intensity of your kicks. To perform this stance, follow the steps given below:

- Stand with your feet together and shift your weight onto one leg.

- Now, set the other leg in front of your body.

- Your foot should not be on the ground. Your toes should only hover slightly above the ground.

- Now use the leg to kick.

Jin Gi Du Li or Golden Rooster Stance

This stance is one-legged and will take you time to perfect. This stance is like the previous stance and serves the same purpose. This stance increases the strength in your legs, thereby making it easier for you to perform kicks. Follow the steps given below to perform this stance:

- Stand with your feet shoulder-width apart.

- Slowly lift your knee. Your toes should point downward at a 45-degree angle.

- Now kick using this leg.

Zuo Dun or Squat Stance

This stance is used when you need to work on your knees. When you perform this stance, you train your knees. To perform this stance, follow the steps given below:

Place Your Feet Shoulder-Width Apart

Lower your body slowly until your knees are at ninety degrees. Your thighs should be parallel to the floor. Keep your back straight.

Try to stay in this position for at least one minute if you are a beginner. Focus on keeping your mind calm when you perform this stance. If you have mastered the stance, you can stay in this position for longer than five minutes. Do not stress your body too much; just start slowly.

Fundamental Footwork

If you have watched someone performing Tai Chi, you will be struck by how beautifully the person performs the art. There is an economy, clarity, control, and grace in every move they make. Many factors come into play when mastering Tai Chi and the different movements in the art. Having said that, when you master fundamental footwork, you can find control and balance. This is fundamental when it comes to Tai Chi. To master Tai Chi, you need to master a few specific movements.

Since Tai Chi has its roots in martial arts, much emphasis is placed on your readiness to react. It is important for you to control and maintain your movements. You need to shift the weight easily from one side of your body to the other with ease while keeping your back straight. These movements are essential if you want to be responsive and maintain balance and stability.

Now compare this to your regular movements. When you walk, you move forward. Your body weight is maintained between the legs. You put one leg in front of the other to avoid falling. When you push a trolley toward the airport's baggage claim, you push your body weight into the trolley to make it move or continue the motion.

The knowledge or understanding your body has about how you should move is very different from the movements you use in Tai Chi. If you want to master Tai Chi, you need to understand how your body should move based on the Tai Chi principles. Since you make subconscious movements in Tai Chi, you are often unaware of whether you conform to the principles. If you are a beginner, this is going to be difficult. There are many things you need to master when it comes to Tai Chi, including:

- The shape of every movement and transition.
- The position of the feet and hands.
- The coordination of the lower and upper body.

You can only focus on the footwork once you are comfortable with the stances and the basic form for Tai Chi. The following are the most important facts to bear in mind when it comes to your footwork:

- You need to move your weight off one foot when you lift your leg.
- Place your foot in front of you before you shift your weight onto it.
- Transfer your weight using your legs.

These points might seem obvious to you, and it is easy to improve if you make an effort.

Shifting Your Weight Off the Foot Before Lifting It

Most daily activities require you to center your weight. It becomes easy to forget about shifting your weight when you move your feet. When you perform a set of Tai Chi exercises, you try to support your weight on one leg only. If you want to maintain control and balance, you need to shift your weight to the supporting leg. Do not place any additional weight on the foot you are about to lift.

Shifting the Weight After Placing Your Foot on the Ground

Martial arts influences this area of footwork. If you perform Tai Chi on slippery or uneven ground, you need to commit and control your weight; otherwise, you will lose balance. If you are not focused and committed to the movement, you need to adjust your stance. If you do not place your foot firmly on the ground before you push any weight onto it, you may experience the following:

- Slamming your foot into the ground when you land.
- Leaning forward while holding the position.
- Maintaining a wider or longer stance that is not comfortable for you.
- Inability to balance.

When you work on maintaining your weight and controlling how you place the weight on your foot, you naturally take shorter steps. You also find yourself in control when you enter or leave a stance. Kicks are the best way to check if you can control the movement of the weight. Once you master the art of landing, you can shift your weight forward. This makes it easier for you to move into the new stance or movement. It is important to maintain your weight when you transition between different movements. You need to check yourself when you move into simpler movements to ensure you are shifting your weight correctly. If you do not focus on your balance when you perform simple stances, you will find it difficult to manage your weight when you move onto harder sets.

Shifting the Weight Using Your Legs

Assume you use a typist chair to support your torso. The chair has wheels at the bottom and moves forward and backward easily. It also comes with a central pole that allows you to shift your body from side to side. When you shift your weight forward, you only need to use your legs. You should avoid using your torso. The leg placed to the front should be relaxed. This means there should be no weight placed on that leg. You should use your back leg to give you the push needed to move the chair forward.

If you use this image, you know you can manage your height level easily. When you perform this movement, you use the muscles in your legs more. This movement tires the muscles in your legs if you perform it correctly. You learn to use your legs more when you perform these functions. You no longer lean your torso forward when you perform this movement.

Once you master these characteristics, you can perform economic, smooth, clean, and clear movements. Make a conscious effort to perform these movements to ensure you do not go back to your previous footwork.

Remember that the classic texts state, "*The energy is routed in the feet, develops in the legs, is directed by the waist, and moves up to the fingers. The feet, legs, and waist must act as one so that when advancing and retreating, you will obtain a good opportunity and a superior position... If you fail to gain these advantages, your body will be in a state of disorder and confusion. The only way to correct this fault is by adjusting your legs and waist.*"

Chapter 7: Hand Movements

Tai Chi is a form of martial arts, both at the lowest and highest levels. You need to adhere to every movement you make and abide by all martial arts principles. Most people make the mistake of looking at Tai Chi as a meditation art. It is important to remember that Tai Chi is a form of martial arts, and you need to study it in this way.

Now that you have this in mind, you will next learn how you can use your hands when you perform Tai Chi. Your hands are your main tools when you interact with your surrounding environment. Your hands hold more than one-quarter of the bones in your body, and around one-fifth of your muscles are used to perform hand movements. When you perform a gesture using your hand, you use at least fifty muscles. There are close to 21,000 sensors of pressure, pain, and heat. You can destroy, heal, and cause pain or pleasure using your hand.

Every tool is designed to perform different tasks. When you use a hammer to sink a nail into a piece of wood, you know it can complete this task. Your hands are designed to do the same as well. They are designed to perform specific movements. Your slender and long fingers can be used to grasp your opponent's hands or fingers. Every part of your hand has been designed for specific functions like tools. You can get the job done in different ways to safeguard yourself.

Bear in mind that you can use your human hand to create different designs. Your hands are limited to a few specific and general tasks, but they have evolved to be used in numerous ways. When you perform Tai Chi, your hands can be used in different ways. You can use variations of these movements to the best of your abilities. You can twist, push, pull, grab, chop, poke, smash, neutralize, slap, strike, adhere, and perform many other movements. Your hands can perform different movements at the same time. You cannot slap your opponent with one finger or grab something with a fist in the same way you cannot cut wood using a hammer. You can use your finger to poke and your fist to punch.

Most Tai Chi practitioners avoid changing their hand postures before they perform different hand movements during their practice. This is a shortcoming since you need to understand how to change hand postures to maintain form. When you change postures, you are letting your body know your intent. Your intent is what drives your practice, and this intent will help you succeed.

The next few sections look at some basic hand positions, their use, and how you can express each of these movements in Tai Chi.

Hand Postures

Normal Hand

This is the simplest and most common hand position used by every Tai Chi practitioner. You maintain this movement when you do not want to perform any movements. This hand is aware of the energy in it. In most martial arts, which use an open hand technique, this hand is called the "at ready" hand. When you hold your hands in a normal position while you wait to do something, it is just relaxing. Most people use this movement to transition between different hand movements. Some examples of where this hand movement is used are the waiting hand used in the Repulse Monkey position or the Fist Under the Elbow.

Tiger's Mouth

This hand movement is used while performing offense moves, including twisting, grabbing, pulling, and neutralizing. The hand movement is open, and there is a lot of space between your index finger and thumb. This movement gives you the ability to clasp and grasp anything between your fingers and thumb. This is an active posture that allows you to twist and grab onto your opponent's arms easily. It is best you do not use this movement when you strike your opponent because it does not do well for strikes. The energy in your palm will be dissipated if you use the movement in a large area. Since your thumb sticks out, your opponent can choose to attack it. Some examples of the use of this movement include the hand used in the High Pat on a Horse, the hand used in the Brush Knee, and the Pulling Hand used in other movements.

Striking Palm

When you perform this hand gesture, hold your thumb close to your palm. Your fingers should be held back slightly and need to be erect. The energy in your palm should be maintained in the lower end of the palm. The bones in the forearm are close to the surface, and you need to protect them from harm. This movement allows you to use the energy found in the palm and project it into your opponent's body. Some examples of this hand movement include Repulse Monkey, Fan Through the Back, and Brush Knee.

Neutralizing and Pushing Hand

This hand movement is used often to either neutralize or push your hand. This is the step between the Tiger's Mouth and relaxed hand movements. You can mold this hand movement in your favor to ensure the movement is soft. This movement allows you to attach the hand to a surface and transmit energy. You need to hold the thumb close to the palm if you want to use the Tiger's Mouth. If you want to use the Striking Palm movement, you need to spread your fingers out slightly. Some examples of this movement include the Withdraw and Push movement, the Push movement, Roll Back and Brush Knee.

Slapping Palm

For this hand movement, you need to keep your hand open. Do not place your thumb on your palm, but only close to it. This hand movement is softer when compared to other hand movements. You can use it to whip your opponent. The objective of this hand movement is not to let the energy penetrate easily. You want to retain your energy. Tai Chi experts often use this movement to confuse their opponents while preparing for other movements. One example of this movement is the High Pat on a Horse, which is discussed in the next section.

Chopping Hand

In this hand movement, you need to hold your fingers firmly together. This motion uses peng energy. Tuck the thumb into your palm, and ensure the energy is focused on the edge of your hand. You can use this energy to chop or move the hand in a downward and upward motion. Some examples of this movement include the upward chop used in the Slanting Flying and the downward chop used in the Deflect Downward movement.

Finger Poke Hand

In this movement, you need to maintain a firm hold. Hold your fingers straight and tuck the thumb into your palm. Your palm, fingers, wrist, and forearm must be in a straight line. When you poke your opponent using this movement, you place excess stress on the joints that are not maintained in a straight line. Some examples of this movement include White Snake Pulls Tongue Out, Needle at the Bottom of the Sea, and Cross Hands.

Striking Using the Back of the Hand

This hand movement is extremely difficult to perform. You need to find a way to master it since the energy used is limited as the bones present in the back of your hand are close to the surface. You may damage or break them easily if you do not use them correctly. You need to use this motion if you want to distract or stun anybody and so, often, your aim will be the person's nose. Fold your fingers to form a ball to ensure the energy is stored in the knuckle area of your hand. One example of this movement is the White Snake.

Fist

You can use the fist in different ways when you perform Tai Chi. You can chop, punch, and use the side, front, or back of your hand. If you use your knuckles, you can use them to protrude or focus energy on your opponent's small areas. One of the most common fist movements used is the straight punch. To perform this movement, you need to close your fist. Do not close it too tightly.

When you punch an opponent, you need to focus on the index and middle fingers. It is only because of the strength in those knuckles that you can throw the strongest punch. Keep your wrist, hand, and forearm in one line to ensure the force only comes from the back of the hand. You need to ensure you do not use your arm badly so that you do not hurt yourself. If your arm is bent at the wrong angle, you do not release all the force in your arm.

You need to use the half twist movement when you perform a punch in Tai Chi. Using this movement allows you to end the motion using your thumb. Keep your palm facing upward and then concentrate and focus on the energy. Do not use a full twist since that will only leave you punching your opponent with your fist facing downward. This will put too much pressure or stress on the tissues connecting your elbow, wrist, and shoulder.

Hook Hand

When you perform the single whip movement, you can use this hand movement. This is a great tool to strike your opponent on the sides. You can also use it to strike them in the wrist area, back of the hand, and knuckles. The hook hand movement can be used to poke your opponent. The movement allows you to focus your energy on small areas of your hand. It also allows you to neutralize the opponent by wrapping your fingers around their wrist. If you learn the yang style of Tai Chi, you will learn ten different types of single whips. You can perform a variation of this movement but try to integrate different hook hands and movements into a single whip.

Tai Chi Movements

The following are some common Tai Chi movements that use the hand movements mentioned above.

Step Back and Repulse Monkey

When you perform this movement, you use the right hand to perform the tiger's mouth and the left hand to strike your palm. This movement allows you to grab your opponent's wrist easily using your right hand. Since they are holding onto your wrist tightly, you need to withdraw your arm slowly until your opponent is close to you. This makes them vulnerable to your strike.

Plane Cross Hands

In this movement, you can use a neutralizing palm. Use the opposite arm as your neutralizing palm. Press your palm slightly downward and toward your opponent's ribs. Use your other arm to poke your opponent. Do not use the tiger's mouth movement if you want to avoid dissipating the energy in the jing.

Single Whip

You can use this movement in different scenarios. When you perform this movement, use the Tiger's Mouth hand gesture to grab your opponent's left wrist. It is best to do this using the opposite hand so that you can strike your opponent in the ribs with your left hand.

White Snake Pulling the Tongue Out

When your opponent is close, you can strike them or protect yourself using your left hand to perform the neutralizing movement. You can then strike your hand against their nose. Use the back of your hand to do this. It is best to strike your opponent on the bridge of their nose since you can cause immense pain without putting in too much effort.

Fan Through Your Back

When your opponent punches you, you can use the Tiger's Mouth movement to grab your opponent's hand. As you pull their hand, you will expose the chest or rib area. You can then strike your opponent with your hand. If you want, you can punch your opponent for better results.

Hitting a Tiger

This movement is interesting and is also known as the Blocking Punch. When you perform this movement, you need to block your opponent's hook punch with your opposite arm. For instance, if your opponent uses his right arm, you need to use your left arm to block the movement. When you block the hook punch, you should also use your right hand to punch your opponent's temple. It will take you some time to learn how to block punches, but once you master them, you will find the movement effective.

Once you finish blocking him, you need to make the next move. Punch your opponent with your right fist in his center. This punch is powerful since you put your entire weight in the punch and use a short range. Some experts use both arms to punch their opponent, but this only comes with practice.

High Pat on Horse

When you perform this movement, you will need to use the tiger's mouth hand gesture to neutralize the movement and slap your opponent's hand. Alternatively, you can use your neutralizing hand to block your opponent's next punch. A slap is quite effective since it adds a slight weight to your opponent's wrist. This will upset their balance and core.

Chapter 8: Tai Chi Warm-Up Exercises

In this chapter, you will look at some warm-up exercises to perform before you practice Tai Chi.

Warm-Up Exercises

The first two steps discussed in this chapter will involve a warm-up and stretching exercise. You need to combine these with Tai Chi movements and practice them regularly if you want to improve your flexibility. These movements will help you tone your muscles.

Before you begin to perform these warm-up exercises and other movements, keep the following points in mind:

- Wear comfortable and loose clothing.
- Ensure your shoes are well-fitting and flat.
- Do not use new movements that cause you pain or discomfort.

- Move only within your comfort range. When you perform a movement for the first time, you need to stretch. Do not stretch your body too much. Start slowly and increase the range slowly.

- Stretch on both sides if you need to.

- Every movement should be performed smoothly and slowly.

You can also choose to do any of the following if you need to:

- Walk around for a few minutes and shake your legs and hands. You can clench and unclench your hands if you want to. This will loosen your joints and body and prepare your body for the movements and exercises you perform.

- You can massage your muscles if you want to. Rub your palms together to generate some energy or qi. Move your palms over your lower back, shoulders, ankles, feet, and legs. Continue to rub your arms together to generate the heat.

- Take a shower or a short walk before you begin your warm-up.

Stretching

Perform the exercises listed in this section at least three times before you begin your workout. There is no sequence you need to follow when it comes to stretching. The following are some points to bear in mind:

- If you cannot balance your body, you can use the wall or a chair to support you.

- Stretch only up to 60 percent of your normal range. You can increase the range slowly if you want to.

You will stretch the most important parts of your body before you perform the movements. You need to stretch your neck, spine, shoulders, knees, ankles, and hips. Since you will only perform two exercises for each part, you can remember them easily. It is important to remember that you will work from the top of your body to the bottom. Keep your feet shoulder-width apart when you perform these exercises unless it is otherwise specified.

Neck

Moving your head back

- Take a deep breath and move your hands up slowly above your head.

- Visualize that two balloons are lifting your wrists slowly.

- Turn your palms to face the wall in front of you. This makes sure your palms point upward.

- Bring your palms toward your chest and push your neck forward. Now, bend your chin backward.

Moving your head down

- Exhale and slowly outstretch your arms in front of you. Extend them fully.

- Now, press your hands down while making sure you do not bend your elbows.

- Slowly move your head toward your chest.

Turning your head

- Lift your right hand to your side and keep your palms facing upward.

- Turn your head to the right and look at the palm. Your left leg should be left at your hip, with your palm facing downward.

- Move your right hand to the right and turn your head while you focus on your palms.

- Now move your face back to the center.

- Perform the same steps with your other hand.

You can perform these exercises as many times as you want to. Release the muscles in your neck.

Shoulders

Rolling your shoulders

You need to roll your shoulders backward and forward to release the muscles. This makes it easier for you to perform movements easily.

Gathering energy

- Take a deep breath and lift your arms to the side. You can keep your elbows soft. Your palms should face upward. Now, move your arms until they curve over your head.

- When you exhale, you need to press your hands downward.

- Move your arms until they are below your belly button.

Spine

Stretching the spine

- Lift your hands in front of you and pretend you are carrying an exercise ball. Inhale deeply.

- Exhale deeply and push your hand upward. Visualize that you are pushing your hand against the wall or ceiling above your head.

- Your fingertips need to face inward.

- While you do this, push your other arm downward and leave your hands by your side.

Switch between your hands.

Twisting your spine

Follow the steps given below to perform this exercise:

- Place your hands in front of you. You need to pretend you are carrying an exercise ball.
- Leave your left leg above your head.
- Bend your knees slightly and turn your waist toward your left.
- The next thing to do is to switch between your hands. Lift the right hand and turn towards the right.
- Your back should be supple and upright.

Hips

Stretching forward

Follow the steps given below to stretch your hip forward:

- Move your left heel in front of your body and slowly push your hands back to maintain balance.
- Now, push your left leg back and rest your body on your toes.
- Stretch your hands forward and lift them to the height of your shoulders.
- Repeat the exercise on the other side.

An alternative to performing this exercise is to step on the toes of your other foot before moving the leg back.

Stretching sideways

- Push your hands to the side and visualize that you are pushing your body against a wall.
- Stretch your opposite foot to the side and stretch.

Knees

Kick

Follow the steps given below to perform this exercise:

- Loosen your fists and set your palms to your side.

- Leave your arms at the sides of your hips.

- Stretch one foot outward and pretend to make a kicking motion.

- While you do this, slowly punch your opposite fist outward. Your palms should face downward.

- Now move your arms and legs back. Repeat this process on the other side.

Stepping forward

- Place your fists close to your hips. Keep your knees relaxed.

- Now, step forward slightly with one foot.

- You can shift your weight onto the front foot.

- As your body moves forward, you need to punch using the opposite arm. You can do the same with the opposite side of the leg.

Ankles

Tapping the ankle

- You need to tap your feet using both your toes and heels.

- Alternate between your legs.

Ankle rotation

With your toes facing downward, lift your heel and move your foot in a clockwise direction thrice. Now, switch to the opposite direction. You can switch between your feet as well.

Chapter 9: The 24-Move Sequence

This chapter will look at a 24-form sequence you need to follow when you perform Tai Chi regularly. The sequence of these movements is:

1. Commencing Form

2. Parting the Horse's Mane

3. White Crane Spreads its Wings

4. Brush Knee

5. Playing the Lute

6. Repulsing the Monkey

7. Grasping the Bird's Tail on the Right

8. Grasping the Bird's Tail on the Left

9. Single Whip

10. Cloud Hands

11. Single Whip

12. High Pat on the Horse

13. Kick Out with the Right Heel

14. Double Punch

15. Turn, Kick Out with the Left Heel

16. Serpent in the Grass on the Right, Golden Cockerel Stands on its Left Leg

17. Serpent in the Grass on the Left, Golden Cockerel Stands on its Right Leg

18. Maiden Working the Shuttles

19. Needle at the Bottom of the Sea

20. Flash Arms like a Fan

21. Turn, Deflect, Parry and Punch

22. Apparent Closing and Push

23. Cross Hands

24. Closing Form

You will now look at how you can perform each of these sequences in the next few sections.

Commencing Form

In this step, you work on your breathing and perform the following Qigong exercises.

Arm Raises

- Place your feet firmly on the ground and shoulder-width apart.

- Spread your weight evenly between your feet.

- Leave your arms to relax at your sides. Do not clench your fists.

- Take a deep breath in and raise your arms to shoulder level. You can move them higher if you feel comfortable.

- Keep your elbows soft and relaxed.

- Now, exhale slowly and lower your arms.

Opening Your Chest

- Stand with your feet firmly placed on the ground while ensuring your weight is spread evenly between your legs.
- Your arms should remain relaxed on either side.
- Take a deep breath and raise your arms to your shoulder level.
- While you exhale, you need to move your arms toward your center while ensuring your palms face each other.
- Move your arms to the middle of your chest. Bear in mind that your shoulders need to be relaxed.
- Now, lower your arms slowly.

Repeat this exercise until you feel relaxed.

Stretching Sideways

- Take a deep breath in and slowly lift your arms above your head. Your elbows should be relaxed and slightly bent. You need to shift your weight on either side.
- Now, lift your opposite arm in front of you and keep it straight. Maintain the position an archer does when they are firing a bow.
- Take another deep breath in and raise both your arms above your head. Now move the weight to the center of your body.
- Breathe out slowly and shift your weight from the right side of your body to the left.
- Mirror this form on the other side.

Repeat this exercise until you feel relaxed.

Bending and Circling Arms

- Stand comfortably on the ground. Maintain a firm form and keep your feet shoulder-width apart. You need to spread your weight evenly.

- Let your arms remain relaxed and loose by your sides.

- Now, cross your hands in front of your body with your palms facing toward you.

- Breathe in deeply and lift your arms above your head as high as you can.

- Now, breathe out and lower your arms slightly. Your elbows should be bent slightly while you return to the center position.

Twisting and swinging your arms

- Turn your body to the right. You should only twist at your waist. You can bend your knees slightly if you need to.

- Take a deep breath in and bend to your right. Move your right arm down the side of your body.

- Your palms should face upward while you move your arm backward in the shape of an arc.

- Lift your elbow to the height of your shoulders.

- Breathe out deeply and rotate your wrists until your palms move forward.

- Now, bring your right arm forward and shift your body weight forward until your arm is in front of you. Move your arms the way you would when you swim.

- Repeat the exercise on the other side.

If you have been practicing Tai Chi for a while, you will know how to perform this movement using both arms. If you are a beginner, you can work with one side at a time to move in the right manner.

Side Arm Rotations

- Take a deep breath in and lift your arms like you are cradling a child or baby.

- Your palms should face you while you turn to the left.

- Now twist your body at the waist to your right and move your weight onto your left foot. Focus on your left arm when you perform this movement.

- Your right hand should always be placed beneath the left arm. Exhale deeply and move back to the center.

- Take another deep breath and move toward your right.

When you perform this movement, the lower arm should always be close to your belly button while the upper arm is away from the middle.

Parting the Horse's Mane

You need to perform this movement three times when you perform Tai Chi. Your weight should be distributed equally between your legs. If you are unsure about how you should maintain your weight equally, follow the steps given below:

- Shift the weight to your left leg by slowly moving off your right leg.

- Lift your heel off the ground until there is no weight placed on your left leg.

- Now, place your leg back on the ground by lowering your toes first.

- Your weight should be distributed evenly between your legs.

To perform this movement, follow the steps given below:

- Stand firmly on the ground and wrap your arms around your thighs. It is best to wrap them around the middle but wrap your arms wherever comfortable if you cannot bend that much.

- Now, use your back muscles to lift your arms. Take a deep breath and move your arms to the chest level.

- Slowly bend downward and exhale deeply. Now, drop your elbows and shoulders using your core and back muscles.

- Now, place your right and left palms close to your belly button like you are holding a ball. The left arm should be placed on the bottom of the ball.

- Shift your legs so that they take the position of the letter T. Place your left foot on your toes to ensure there is no weight on the leg. Move your weight onto the right foot.

- Your right hand should be at your chest while your left hand is close to your belly button. Now, curve your fingers like you are holding the ball.

- Place your left foot now on its heel and maintain a 90-degree angle.

- Your left hand should move along with the left leg.

- Keep your knees open and flared.

- Your head should always be erect, and the weight should move to the center of your body.

- You need to move your left hand at the same time you move your hips. This will help you shift your weight evenly between your legs to maintain your posture.

- Now, stretch the knee of your right leg to ensure you do not flex or strain your back.

- Sit down until your left leg is on the heel and the weight shifts to the back foot. Now, flex your right knee, so your buttocks, back, and head are maintained in the same line.

- Next, pivot your heel until your leg is at a 45-degree angle. You need to align your hip and shift your weight onto the left foot. Now, align your hips.

- Step out of the position at a 90-degree angle and move the left hand toward the leg. Your fingers should be aligned together and away from the thumb.

- Move your hand toward the front of your body and open the palm slowly like you are serving your horse a meal.

- Move your right hand to your side and bend the elbow. The finger should be curved or rounded like you are holding the top of a ball. Your legs and hands should move simultaneously when you perform the movement.

- Now, sit down until your front foot is on the heel, but the weight is only on the back foot. Flex your knee to ensure your buttocks and back are maintained in a straight line.

White Crane Spreads Its Wings

To perform this exercise, follow the steps given below:

- Move your right step slightly forward. Do not place any weight on the right leg.

- Pretend you are holding onto a ball, but do not place any weight on your toes. Place your right hand at the bottom of the ball and your left hand on top.

- Now rotate or spin the ball while slowly shifting your weight from the front leg to the back leg. The ball should move in a counterclockwise direction.

- Lift your right hand upward and move it above your head. Your little finger should be in a position that allows you to cut the edge of the shoulder. Now, leave your hand in a relaxed form.

- Move the left hand to your side and maintain it in a cocked position. You need to bend the elbow and ensure your fingers are curved like they are placed on the top of the ball.

• Slowly shift your weight to the foot placed in the back. At the same time, you need to perform the following movements:

  • Sit down on your right foot.

  • Bend your left hand slightly at the elbow.

  • Place your left hand with the little finger pointing outward.

Brush Knee

To perform this stance, you need to follow the steps given below. You will perform this stance first using the left leg.

• Stand with your feet shoulder-distance apart and maintain a firm grip on the ground.

• Move your left foot until it faces the wall in front of you. The right foot should be pointed diagonally.

• Now, bend both your knees slightly and shift your weight to the front. Do not shift the full weight, but only 70 percent of your weight.

• Press your right hand forward and let your palm face the front wall. Leave your left hand on the thigh and relax.

• Now move your weight onto the right leg, which is at the back, and sit down on the leg. Shift your weight onto this leg.

• Your hands should remain in the same position but slowly expand. Do not turn your body at your waist.

• Now, turn your body at the waist toward your left. Let the left leg relax and turn outward to the left on your toes while your waist turns. Your palms should face you. Do not let your weight shift.

- Move your hips forward and shift the weight as well. Slowly move your hips diagonally and move the knee in. Push your right foot to the front and move your hips into a diagonal position.

- Shift the weight onto the left leg and maintain it until your right foot is off the floor. Then, move the right knee forward to meet the left knee.

- The right hand should now be at the center of your chest. Hold your arms like you are holding a ball.

- The left arm should move in line with your body. Leave the palms facing downward and at shoulder height. Do not turn your waist, but shift your weight diagonally.

- Now move your right leg, which does not have any weight on it, to the right side of your body. Do not move your weight in this step.

- Lower your right arm slowly and straighten the left arm until your palm faces upward. Now, bend your left elbow slowly and point your fingers to your ears.

- Turn your waist slightly toward the front wall but make sure not to shift your weight.

- Move your waist forward and shift your weight onto your right leg back to the initial weight shift.

- Lower your right hand until your hand is close to your leg. Let your hand rest against your thigh.

- Now, move the left arm until it is in front of you and turn the waist slowly while your palm faces the front of the shoulder.

You need to perform this exercise thrice.

Playing the Lute

Follow the steps given below to perform this exercise:

- When you perform this movement, you need to step forward. You need to move the right foot in front of you without placing too much weight on the leg. Move your right foot until you stand on your toes.

- Move the left hand above your head and keep it slightly bent.

- Now, move the right hand until your fingers are aligned to the left elbow. Bend the right hand slightly at the elbow and turn it inward. Do not maintain it parallel to the left hand.

- Move your weight slowly to the back leg. Your left leg may be a little wobbly when you start. You need to lift the heel off the ground and sit down carefully on your leg.

- Set the left heel firmly on the ground.

- Your hands need to be set in the right position, where your right hand is in line with the left elbow and is maintained in an inward position.

- Firmly place your heels on the ground while you shift your weight onto your left leg. Crouch by dropping your shoulders.

- Always maintain your balance and posture.

Repulsing the Monkey

Once you have performed the previous movement three times, move onto this movement. To perform this movement, follow the steps given below:

- Stand with your feet shoulder-width apart and place your heels firmly on the ground. Your weight should be distributed evenly between the legs.

- Move your left hand to the center of your body and shift your right hand to the back. Try to maintain a 90-degree angle using your right hand.

- Turn your neck and face toward the right hand as you move it.

- Keep your palms open and ensure they face upward at the same time.

- Now, look at your right hand and keep it higher than the left hand. Now turn your head and neck to follow the back hand as you move it.

- Lift your right hand higher than your left hand.

- While you do this, you need to move your weight onto your back leg. To do this, you need to move your front leg and lift it slightly.

- Now, stretch or extend your knee as you bring the leg back. You need to position the toe out and back so the leg is not on the same line as the front foot.

- Lower the toes until they are away from the front foot and turn the heel inward. Try to maintain a 45-degree angle.

- Move the back hand closer to the ear and follow the movement of the hand using your head.

- While you do this, you need to move the right foot forward to meet the center. Move your hands to the center while you push and pull them away from each other.

- The hand moving forward should always be at the center of the body. Your fingers should be curved, and your palms must face outward.

- Let your left hand move back while you curve the palm.

- Open the left hand and move it to your hip.

- Now, stretch the knee of your front leg and lower your body onto the back leg. Shift your weight slowly and carefully onto your leg to prevent any injury.

- Face the front when you perform this movement.

Repeat this movement on the other side. Before you do this, shift the weight to the center.

Grasping the Bird's Tail on the Right and Left

To perform this movement, follow the steps given below. Bear in mind that the steps to perform this movement on both the right and left sides are the same. You will look at how you can perform this movement on your left.

- You need to pivot your right foot using your heel.

- Now move your left foot away from the right foot, which will remain at the back.

- Hold the ball with your left hand on top and right hand at the bottom. You can shift the bottom hand toward your body to ensure your palms face you.

- Rotate your body and flip your hands. The hand at the bottom should face the upper hand.

- Lower both hands at the same time and make sure they are equidistant.

- Move your head backward and look at your hands as you move them toward the back. Now, rotate your body and square your waist and hips while you move your hands forward.

- When your right hand and left wrist meet, you can push your arms out and separate them.

- Sit back on your left leg slowly and shift your body weight onto the back leg. Now push your body forward and lower your left hand. Use your left heel to pivot your leg.

- Move back to the center and hold the ball as you maintain a T-step.

Single Whip

You have looked at how you can perform the movement in the previous chapter. You need to complete this movement at least three times on either side after performing the bird's tail.

Cloud Hands

To perform this movement, follow the steps given below:

- Stand with your feet facing the front and placed shoulder-width apart. Visualize that your head is being lifted from your crown

- Tuck your chin toward your chest and look forward. Relax your body and let your arms hang loose at your sides.

- Part your fingers gently and curve them slightly.

- Your palms should not face away from your body.

- Your tailbone should be tucked inward and your knees bent slightly.

- Now, breathe in slowly and turn your left arm to face your body. Hold your palm in line with the center of your chest and facing inward.

- Your left elbow should be maintained at the same level or below your left hand. Curve the fingers slightly inward.

- When you do this, you need to extend your right arm and maintain it at the height of your waist.

- Turn your right palm downward and curve your fingers slightly. Keep your elbows bent.

- Shift your weight slowly to the left leg while you turn your waist slowly. Your arms should follow your waist as you turn.

- Now, turn your right palm to face your body while you curve the fingers. Your left palm should face downward and the fingers need to point forward. You can curve them if you want to.

- Raise your right arm until it is at your shoulder's level and slowly lower your left hand until it is at your waist.

- Exhale and turn your body back to the center while you transfer the weight.

- Breathe in deeply and transfer the weight onto your right leg while turning your body to the right. Turn your arms along with your waist.

- Now, turn the left palm inward to face the body while you curve your fingers.

- The right palm should face downward with your fingers curved slightly. Lift the left arm to the height of your shoulders and drop the right hand to your waist.

- Now, breathe out slowly and twist your body back to the center. Shift your weight to the center when you do this.

- Take another deep breath in and perform the exercise eight times.

Once you finish the repetitions, you can move back to the starting position. Breathe out and let your arms relax at your sides.

High Pat on the Horse

You have looked at how you can perform the movement in the previous chapter. You can take a break before you perform this exercise if you are tired. You need to remember that your body is not used to this type of workout, and you may tire easily.

Kick Out with the Right and Left Heel

The following are some types of kicks you can perform with your heels.

Reverse Kick

When you perform this kick, you need to move backward while keeping the leg you want to kick with close to the standing leg. Since you are looking at kicking using the right heel, you need to move the right leg close to the left leg. Use your heel to strike the opponent. You need to deliver the kick by stepping backward. This type of kick is damaging since it uses a lot of power.

Type One

- Breathe in deeply and keep your feet shoulder-width apart. Relax your arms on either side of your body.

- Turn your body to the left and throw your right leg backward.

- Now, shift your weight onto your left leg and lift your right heel to hit the groin.

Type Two

- Breathe in deeply and keep your feet shoulder-width apart. Relax your arms on either side of your body.

- Turn your body to the left and throw your right leg backward.

- Now, shift your weight onto your left leg and lift your right heel to hit the shin.

Side Kick

The side kick is another movement you can perform. You need to shift your weight and move your body sideways. When you perform this movement, you can use two areas as the points of impact. You can use the heel or the outer edge of your foot to perform this movement. This movement is often used as an offensive movement in Tai Chi since it can damage your opponent.

Type One

- Breathe in deeply and keep your feet shoulder-width apart. Relax your arms on either side of your body.

- Lift your hands to block your chest.

- Now, shift your body weight to the left and slowly raise the right leg to the side and kick at the person's shin or heel.

Type Two

- Breathe in deeply and keep your feet shoulder-width apart. Relax your arms on either side of your body.

- Lift your hands to block your chest.

- Now, shift your body's weight to the left and slowly raise the right leg to the side and kick at the person's knee.

You need to perform this movement using your right heel before you move onto the double punch movement. Then move onto performing the exercise using your left heel.

Double Punch

To perform this movement, follow the steps given below:

- Stand with your feet shoulder-width apart and move your right leg in front of the left.

- Now, shift your weight gently from the back foot to the front.

- Create a fist using both hands and push both arms out in front of you. Push your right arm in front before your left arm.

- Now, shift your weight onto the back leg and pivot your feet around.

The Serpent in the Grass on the Right, Golden Cockerel Stands on Its Left Leg

When you finish kicking out with your left heel, you can perform this movement. Follow the steps given below to do this:

- You need to bring your serpent in. Stand with your feet firmly on the ground and hook your right hand. Shift this hand above the left hand and look at it.

- Move your right leg to the front and slowly shift your weight onto the back leg.

- Now, lower your body halfway and slowly shift your weight.

- Shift your body slightly and pivot using both feet. You can perform the serpent movement on the other side.

Perform this movement at least thrice on both sides.

The remaining movements, listed below, are easy to perform. The names clearly define how you need to perform these movements. It is important to remember how to balance your body and weight when you perform the following.

Maiden Working the Shuttles

To perform this movement, follow the steps mentioned below:

- Place your feet shoulder-width apart and relax your arms at your sides.

- Now, shift your right heel out and extend the knee.

- Move your hand to the right and shift your waist and hips.

- Shift your foot outward and then move your hand.

- Move your hand forward and back above your forehead while you breathe in and out (this is like moving a shuttlecock above your head).

- Lower your hand below and rotate your waist and hips.

- Now lower your body slowly onto the back leg and shift your weight onto the leg.

- Hold your hands in front of you as if you are holding a ball and push your legs in.

- Perform the same exercise with your other leg.

Repeat this movement three times before you move onto the next movement.

Needle at the Bottom of the Sea

To perform this step, follow the steps given below:

- Stand with your feet shoulder-width apart and move your arms back.

- Now, slowly lift your left leg. Lift it high enough so that your big toe touches the ground.

- Bend your right knee slightly and maintain the position.

- Lift your right hand and move it toward the left knee.

- Bend down slowly and reach toward the left big toe to find the needle.

- Slowly move your hand back up and straighten your back.

- Now, lower your foot and relax.

Repeat this exercise with your right leg.

Flash Arms Like a Fan

Once you repeat the previous movement three times on either side, you can relax before starting this movement.

- Stand with your feet shoulder-width apart. Let your hands relax on your thighs.

- Now, bend your right knee slightly and shift your weight onto the right leg.

- Lift your arms and keep the elbows bent.

- Stretch the back knee out as far as you can and lower yourself on your right leg.

- Come out of the position by releasing your arms and slowly moving your weight back to your center.

- Repeat this exercise with your left leg.

Turn, Deflect, Parry, and Punch

After performing the previous movement, you should come back to your center of balance before performing this movement.

- Stand with your feet shoulder-width apart and relax your arms at your sides. Slowly lift your arms upward and maintain them in front of you. Ensure the palms face away from you.

- Now, place your left foot forward and bend the knees slightly. Lift your left arm and maintain it parallel to your thigh. Lift your right arm and keep it underneath your left arm.

- Slowly shift your weight from the right leg onto the left by moving your back forward.

- Turn left using your hips and waist.

- Lift your right leg and move through the left leg. Now, your right leg is in front of you. Land on your heel. You need to move your arms the same way you did in step two, but with opposite hands.

- Turn to your right and move your left leg in front of your right leg. Now, slowly move back to the center.

When you perform this movement, you need to shift your weight slowly onto the leg you are placing in front of you. This is the only way you can maintain your balance throughout the movement.

The last two movements are the apparent closing and pushing. These movements are of utmost importance since you will use all the energy in your body. The pushing movement and how it works are explained in the next chapter.

Once you perform these movements, you can close off the form and stretch. Center your weight and balance yourself in the right position.

Chapter 10: Pushing Hands: Eight Gates and Five Steps

Push hands is an important practice performed when you practice Tai Chi. When you perform this movement, you need to use the four directions, and it is best to perform this movement with someone else. If you use local strength or muscle, you cannot train using the energies in the four directions. When you perform this movement, you always need to maintain the energy. You also need to manifest the energy from different directions whenever your partner touches you. It is important to keep yourself relaxed when you do this.

The energy in your arms and hands is manipulated by the movements you make. You can easily work with this energy and manipulate it when you move your waist. To do this, you need to relinquish the control you exert from your shoulders and arms and relax your shoulders. It is only when you do this that the movement will have the necessary effects.

It is hard for you to control your arms using your waist since this is not something you are used to. You also need to let your waist control the way you move. You can start with the pushing hand movement using a single hand. You will move on to using both hands to perform this exercise in the next few steps. You need to practice the pattern carefully and fix the way you move before moving your arms freely. Practice this movement carefully.

Assume you are in combat. You may find yourself in a position where you are going to lose. It is during this time that you need to step out and let your partner win. Do not resist the win because that only leads to tension in the muscles. You may begin to use your local muscles to do this, which you need to stop. Do not develop any bad habits that could lead you away from using the energy in your body. Invest and learn from your losses.

When you are in combat, you need to ensure your opponent does not come too close to you. If you can control your opponent's direction and center, you can let them approach you. Most people lose in combat Tai Chi because they let their opponent enter their space without maintaining any control. When you perform Tai Chi, whether in combat or practice, you need to maintain some connection with the energy—this is the only way you can match your opponent.

Whenever you connect with your opponent, you need to ensure the contact is light. You should never try to hurt your opponent unless you are defending yourself. When you are in combat, learn to focus on your opponent's balance. Never let your arms and hands move too far away. They need to be close to your center. Never focus on your local muscles but consider your entire body.

Use your leg strength during combat. This is a way to overpower your opponent. If your legs are strong, you can source your power and energy from your lower body. When your source of energy is lower and stronger, you can push your hands easily and effectively. You need to monitor how you feel and how pure your energy is. You also need to check if you are relaxed or not and identify the areas that may have forced you to use too much strength. Learn to correct these movements to avoid any mistakes in the future. As mentioned earlier, you need to use the energy from your legs when you perform Tai Chi. You will soon learn to move away from people easily.

Eight Gates and Five Steps

When you perform Tai Chi, you need to control, cultivate, and unify your body's energy with the energy of the universe. This vital and primary energy in your body is termed qi. When you move, the muscles in your body use a form of energy termed li. This energy is bioelectric and is a purely physical form of energy. When you learn to combine the universal, primal energy with the physical energy, you develop energy in your body called jing or jen. This is the energy that powers every move you make is Tai Chi. The postures discussed in the previous chapter are powered by this energy only.

Most of the postures require much footwork. It is only when you manage to maintain your footwork that you can move your body smoothly from one posture to another. You can also maintain balance only when you manage your footwork. There are five steps used in each of these postures, and these are termed as the five steps. These patterns include the following steps:

- Maintaining central equilibrium
- Stepping forward
- Stepping backward
- Turning right
- Turning left

The other postures you maintain will help you determine how you express or use jing when you fight. These postures are termed as the eight gates or eight energies. You can connect these energies to the Tai Chi compass. You can divide these eight energies into four directions or four primary energies and four corners or four secondary energies. The primary energies are known as:

- Roll back
- Push
- Press forward
- Ward off

The secondary energies are known as:

- Shoulder stroke
- Elbow stroke
- Split
- Pull down

Every movement you make in Tai Chi is based on these blocks. You need to learn how to move continuously and smoothly between each of these blocks. When you master these blocks, you can combine, split, and recombine the movements until you find a sequence that works for you.

Chapter 11: Combat Tactics and Sequences

An important aspect to bear in mind is that Tai Chi is a martial art. You need to understand different fighting strategies to ensure you are not on the losing team. Wait for your enemy to attack your first, so you get to make the first contact. The following are some points to bear in mind.

Focus on Timing, Movement, and Distance

If you want to ensure your opponent attacks first, you need to maintain the right distance between yourself and the opponent. You also need to time your movements. It is also important for you to learn more about Tai Chi before choosing to fight with anybody else. Tai Chi refers to the use of energy and minimizing the number of movements you make.

Understanding the Physical Strategy

From what you have read, you should understand that Tai Chi is a moving martial art. It is important for you to learn how to use space and distance easily. You can use kicks or punches to determine the distance between yourself and your opponent. Understanding this is the essence or foundation of the strategy of Tai Chi. You should walk out of your attacker's range or enter it only when you know you can change the outcome to your advantage. Consider the following scenario to help you understand the same:

- Your enemy is around ten feet from you.

- You know they need to cover this distance if they want to attack you.

- This gives you enough time to plan your counterattack when your attacker moves toward you.

- You can hit your opponent before they reach you, as well.

Land the First Hit

Another way to look at the above scenario is that you invite your opponent to move into your attack zone so that you can evade their strikes. You only need to wait patiently to do this. When they enter your attack zone, you can strike them easily at their weakest point. If you are unsure of their weak point, you can pick your best movement and strike the attacker with the required speed. If your attacker moved carefully and struck you first, it is important to bear in mind that you took the last hit.

End the Fight with Little Force

The objective of every Tai Chi fight should be to end it without confronting the attacker with too much force. You only need to prevent the attacker from finding anywhere to strike.

Move Carefully

Consider how you would hang a shower curtain or towel. When you strike a shower curtain or towel very hard and fast, it will only bend or move. Do you think you can put a hole in this curtain or towel? If you have watched the karate kid movie starring Jackie Chan and Jaden Smith, you know this is quite possible. You cannot expect the towel or curtain to give away unless you make the required effort.

You need to look at how energy flows when you make any movement compared to how the curtain or towel moves. This will give you an idea of how you want your movements to flow and transition. Do you think you can be soft to ensure nobody can hit you and cause harm? You can do this, but you will need to practice to know how you can move in this way.

Become Hard

When you want to attack your opponent, you need to become a solid object. This is the only way you can use your body weight to transmit all your energy to attack your opponent.

Throw in Some Yin and Yang

If you move from a flowing and soft motion like a shower curtain or towel to a connected and solid piece, you will learn to display the concept of yin and yang when you fight. Relax before you start the fight and wait until you want to strike your opponent. When your opponent is close to you, see how you can transfer the weight in one strike.

Chapter 12: Daily Tai Chi Practice

The movements of Tai Chi are gentle, flowing, and smooth. Through these movements, you learn to treat your body to a relaxing and gentle workout. You can say goodbye to workouts that make you pant, puff, and sweat. You will feel energized, refreshed, cool and calm after a Tai Chi workout. Spend only fifteen minutes every day if you want to improve your fitness, health, and peace of mind. You have looked at the benefits of Tai Chi earlier in the book, and you can reap these benefits if you perform Tai Chi for at least ten minutes every day. You will see that your body and mind work in harmony.

You can try the different Tai Chi exercises and Qigong exercises mentioned in this book. They are fun, and you should enjoy performing them, too. You can perform a relaxing Tai Chi exercise if you are stressed or having a terrible day at work. The following are some tips you need to bear in mind if you want to integrate Tai Chi into your workout and daily routine.

Tips

Be Open

The first thing to bear in mind is to keep yourself open to the energy of the universe. You need to learn to develop this connection between everything in your surrounding environment. Learn to relax.

Observe Nature

When you perform Tai Chi exercises, you focus on your breathing and the surrounding environment. You need to observe everything happening in nature around you. Focus on the wind, rain, sun, and stillness. Notice how the energy is flowing from one entity to the next around you.

Be Aware of Your Connection

You should become aware of where you are seated. Find your connection with the ground and develop on that connection. According to Huang Sheng-Shyan, "*If you practice (a martial art) without paying attention to your gong (base), then it will be a lifetime of empty practice.*"

Find the Connection to Your Whole Body

You need to learn how to let the energy from within you flow through your consciousness. Let the movement of this energy rise from the source within you. According to Wee Kee-Jin, "*Moving the arms is not Tai Chi - your arms do move, but they move dependent upon initiation of movement from the base, not on their own.*"

Be Consistent

As with any other exercise regime or workout, you need to be consistent if you want to make steady progress.

Practice with People

If you know you cannot do it alone, you can work with someone who supports you and your aspirations. Speak to a friend or your family and see if anybody is willing to perform Tai Chi with you. Choose a friend or family member who will support you and help you maintain discipline. If you are conscious about doing it alone, take someone with you.

Either Workout Barefoot or Wear Thin Shoes

You need to find a way to connect to the earth. To do this, you can either wear thin-soled shoes or perform Tai Chi barefoot. You can buy Tai Chi shoes if you need to, which allow you to connect easily to the earth and make it easier for the earth's energy to move throughout your body. You can wear softer shoes regularly to continue to feel the energy from the earth.

Learn to Forgive

When you perform Tai Chi, you try to rid your body of any toxic energy. You need to let your heart and mind let go of the past and toxic memories. This enables you to focus on the present and accept the future with an open mind. Forgive yourself and people for any bad memories from the past.

Focus on Your Movements

You need to shift your energy and weight when you perform any Tai Chi movement. You have looked at this in detail in the book. Pay attention to your every movement throughout the day. This helps you determine how the energy flows in your body.

Identify the Yin and Yang in You

As a Tai Chi practitioner, you need to find the Yin and Yang energies within you. Each of these energies contains the other. Find the balance between these energies and in your life. Accept yourself for who you are.

Chapter 13: What to Expect from Your First Class

If you choose to take a Tai Chi class to master the movements and footwork, you need to keep some points in mind. It is important to remember that Tai Chi classes will vary because of the location, instructor, and the Tai Chi style you are practicing. Now, look at some things you can expect from the class.

Meditative and Quiet Surroundings

When you work out with a large group of people, you tend to work in a gym or at a fitness center. The place is always noisy and bustling since people enter and leave after their workout. These places have upbeat music playing. Tai Chi is a very different art form, and it is meditative in nature. You need to find yourself in a quiet and calm environment if you want to practice Tai Chi. Most instructors choose to hold Tai Chi classes outdoors, but this is not always possible. If classes are held indoors, there is no loud music to interrupt your thoughts. The environment is soft and quiet. Every participant is also expected to respect the environment and maintain calm.

A Diverse Group

Anyone can perform Tai Chi. This means there is no age restriction. When you enter a class, you may find people from all walks of life around you, which should not surprise you. You need to embrace diversity because Tai Chi classes are different from regular fitness classes.

You can enroll yourself in a Tai Chi class if you are a beginner or an expert. If you are a beginner, you may feel overwhelmed when you find some members doing better than you. This should not worry you because you will improve over time. When you enter your class, choose a spot where you are comfortable and focus on the movements and energy flow. Focus on what the instructor has to say to you.

Nobody in class will look at you because each member is focusing only on their movements. You do not have to feel awkward. You may find people around you who will help you if you need to correct your movement.

Introduction to Tai Chi

Your instructor will tell you a little bit about Tai Chi before you start the class if you are a beginner. Most instructors do not give you much information about what Tai Chi is, but this book has everything you need to know. An instructor will expect you to have some idea about what Tai Chi is and will work on expanding that knowledge.

Warm-Up

It is important to warm your body up before you perform any exercise. You need to perform each warm-up exercise carefully since these exercises prepare your body for the movements you will make during the class. Tai Chi is a full-body workout, and it makes sense for you to prepare for the session. Most warm-up sessions use easy and gentle motions. Some exercises may include pacing, walking, rotating your shoulders, moving your head in either direction, clenching your hands, rocking on your toes, and more. It is during this time that you need to move into the right headspace. You need to clear your emotions and thoughts. Let go of any stress by preparing your mind to concentrate on the task at hand.

Breathing Exercises

You have looked at the importance of breathing when it comes to Tai Chi, and this is something every instructor will make you do at the start of the class. It is important to learn to breathe slowly and deeply when you perform Tai Chi. When you learn to breathe in this way, you relax both your mind and body. It also becomes easier to focus on your energy or qi. An instructor may choose one of the different meditation techniques discussed in the book.

Stretches

Before you begin to perform the different movements, you need to stretch your body's muscles to loosen them up, just like you do with most sports. An instructor can choose to perform easy to intense warm-up exercises depending on the movements being performed in class. You have looked at a few stretches you can perform at the start of the class for your knees, spine, hip, neck, and shoulders. You can repeat these stretches until you feel relaxed.

Instruction of Movements

This is the main part of your class since you learn the different forms and movements in Tai Chi. At the start of the class, the instructor will show you a few combinations or groups of movements. You may hear strange names being called out while depicting a certain movement. It is easier to use these names since they depict the exact movement you need to perform. There are different combinations and drills you can ask the instructor to teach you.

Repetition of Movements

When the instructor has taught students the movements and demonstrated each movement's flow, they will repeat it for you. They will also expect you to follow them as they repeat the movements. They may walk around the class and correct students who have trouble with performing some of the movements. If you are struggling with any form or movement, you can ask your instructor for further assistance. In Tai Chi, you must learn how to perform every movement correctly. It will take some time to master these movements and forms. If you are practicing Tai Chi for the first time, you may feel slightly disoriented after class. The trick is to stick with the practice so that you improve over time.

Relaxation and Cool Down

Regardless of the type of exercise you perform, you need to cool down and relax the muscles used during the workout. You need to spend some time breathing and stretching at the end of a Tai Chi class. Some instructors use this time to speak to you about applying different movements and techniques in your everyday life. At the end of the class, you will notice that you are more connected to your environment than before. While you cool down, try to focus on the different areas in your life where you can use the movements you performed in class. After you have cooled down, spend some time talking with the people around you.

Socialize

Many people join a club or class because they want to meet new people. When you are in a Tai Chi class, you cannot chat with your neighbors in class. You can mingle with them after class for a short while if you have the time. It is best to learn more about your group during this time. You will also make a lot of friends. Since you spend a few hours with these people every week, you will feel better when you learn more about them.

You can also speak to the instructor to learn more about them if you need to. You can talk to them about any issues or difficulties you may have with some of the movements. Since Tai Chi is a meditative martial art form, you need some time to adjust to your life after class. So, take this time after class to adjust and go back to your work.

Conclusion

If you are new to Tai Chi, you may not know that Tai Chi is a martial arts technique that originated in China. This art is an internal martial art, and it uses round, soft, and slow movements. Through Tai Chi, you will learn to redirect your energy and your opponent's energy through simple movements.

This book should have left you with information about what Tai Chi is and how it benefits you. It also shed some light on the different movements in Tai Chi and how you can master those movements. The book also gave you some Qigong exercises to perform before you begin the sequence of movements. If you follow the instructions in the book carefully, you can improve your overall health and wellbeing.

Since Tai Chi is a form of martial arts, you need to learn how to defend yourself. You also need to have some tricks up your sleeve to ensure you beat your opponent when you spar. This book has some tips and strategies you can use to help you to defeat your opponent.

Thank you for purchasing the book. Hopefully, you develop a habit to practice Tai Chi regularly to improve your mental, physical, spiritual, and emotional wellbeing.

Here's another book by Mari Silva that you might like

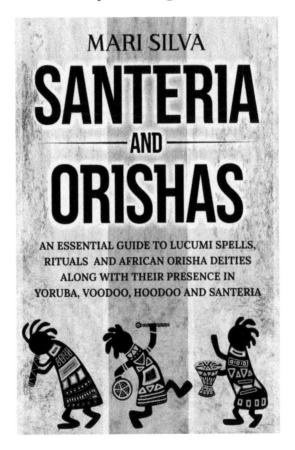

Your Free Gift (only available for a limited time)

Thanks for getting this book! If you want to learn more about various spirituality topics, then join Mari Silva's community and get a free guided meditation MP3 for awakening your third eye. This guided meditation mp3 is designed to open and strengthen ones third eye so you can experience a higher state of consciousness. Simply visit the link below the image to get started.

https://spiritualityspot.com/meditation

References

Byrne, K. (2017, June 1). A Brief History of Tai Chi in China. Culture Trip. https://theculturetrip.com/asia/china/articles/a-brief-history-of-tai-chi-in-china/

Caldwell, K. L., Bergman, S. M., Collier, S. R., Triplett, N. T., Quin, R., Bergquist, J., & Pieper, C. F. (2016). Effects of Tai Chi chuan on anxiety and sleep quality in young adults: lessons from a randomized controlled feasibility study. Nature and science of sleep, 8, 305–314. https://www.dovepress.com/effects-of-tai-chi-chuan-on-anxiety-and-sleep-quality-in-young-adults--peer-reviewed-fulltext-article-NSS

Chan, A. W., Yu, D. S., Choi, K. C., Lee, D. T., Sit, J. W., & Chan, H. Y. (2016). Tai Chi qigong as a means to improve night-time sleep quality among older adults with cognitive impairment: a pilot randomized controlled trial. Clinical interventions in aging, 11, 1277–1286. https://www.dovepress.com/tai-chi-qigong-as-a-means-to-improve-night-time-sleep-quality-among-ol-peer-reviewed-fulltext-article-CIA

Every day Tai Chi. (n.d.). Everydaytaichi.org. http://www.everydaytaichi.org/

Five Steps and Eight Energies - Tai Chi Transformation. (n.d.). Taichitransformation.com. http://taichitransformation.com/primal13_energy.php

Frantzis, B. (2010, September 16). Tai Chi Meditation. Energy Arts. https://www.energyarts.com/tai-chi-meditation/

FUNDAMENTAL FOOTWORK. (n.d.). Www.taichiaustralia.com. https://www.taichiaustralia.com/articles/Fundamental_Footwork.htm

Harvard Health Publishing. (2019, August 20). The health benefits of Tai Chi - Harvard Health. Harvard Health; Harvard Health. https://www.health.harvard.edu/staying-healthy/the-health-benefits-of-tai-chi

Heel Kick (Taijiquan Movement). (n.d.). Modern Wushu Wiki. https://modern-wushu.fandom.com/wiki/Heel_Kick_(Taijiquan_Movement)

Helmer, J. (n.d.). Tai Chi and Qi Gong: Better Balance and Other Benefits. WebMD. https://www.webmd.com/fitness-exercise/a-z/tai-chi-and-chi-gong

History of Tai Chi. (n.d.). Www.seas.ucla.edu. http://www.seas.ucla.edu/spapl/qifeng/history.html

How Tai Chi Breathing Can Make You Better, Faster, Stronger. (2017, March 29). Openfit. https://www.openfit.com/tai-chi-breathing-how-to-benefits

Hui, S. S.-C., Xie, Y. J., Woo, J., & Kwok, T. C.-Y. (2015, October 12). *Effects of Tai Chi and Walking Exercises on Weight Loss, Metabolic Syndrome Parameters, and Bone Mineral Density: A Cluster Randomized Controlled Trial.* Evidence-Based Complementary and Alternative Medicine. https://www.hindawi.com/journals/ecam/2015/976123/

Integrate Tai Chi into Your Daily Routine - Acufinder.com. (n.d.). Acufinder.com.

https://www.acufinder.com/Acupuncture+Information/Detail/Integr
ate+Tai+Chi+into+Your+Daily+Routine

Jerry. (2019, May 25). What is the Dantian? Balanced Life Tai Chi.
https://balancedlifetaichi.com/blog/so02csj1tgsp74hlwwlk6en8ybjv1
9

Lam, P. (2014, January 28). History of Tai Chi. Tai Chi for Health
Institute. https://taichiforhealthinstitute.org/history-of-tai-chi-2/

LaMeaux, E. C. (n.d.). 4 Tai Chi Meditation Techniques. Gaiam.
https://www.gaiam.com/blogs/discover/4-tai-chi-meditation-
techniques

Li, F., Harmer, P., Fitzgerald, K., Eckstrom, E., Stock, R., Galver,
J., Maddalozzo, G., & Batya, S. S. (2012). Tai Chi and Postural
Stability in Patients with Parkinson's Disease. New England Journal
of Medicine, 366(6), 511–519.
https://www.nejm.org/doi/full/10.1056/NEJMoa1107911

Mortazavi, H., Tabatabaeichehr, M., Golestani, A., Armat, M. R., &
Yousefi, M. R. (2018). The Effect of Tai Chi Exercise on the Risk
and Fear of Falling in Older Adults: a Randomized Clinical Trial.
Materia socio-medica, 30(1), 38–42.
https://www.ejmanager.com/mnstemps/16/16-
1518555232.pdf?t=1623002592

Nordqvist, J. (2018, August 30). Tai Chi: Benefits, types, and
history. Www.medicalnewstoday.com.
https://www.medicalnewstoday.com/articles/265507

Sauer, M. (2018, May 14). Tai Chi Benefits: Stress Reduction,
Weight Loss, for Older Adults. Healthline.
https://www.healthline.com/health/tai-chi-benefits#arthritis

Shojai, P. (2019, January 6). What is Qi Gong? Your Guide to This
Asian Yoga Practice. Yoga Journal.
https://www.yogajournal.com/yoga-101/what-is-qi-gong/

Signam, M. (n.d.). Guidelines for Pushing Hands by Mike Sigman. Www.wooddragon.org.uk. http://www.wooddragon.org.uk/tai_chi_push_hands.html

Tai Chi: Definition and History - Tai Chi Association Colorado Springs, LLC. (2012, June 3). Tai Chi Association Colorado Springs, LLC. https://taichicoloradosprings.com/tai-chi-definition-and-history/

Tai Chi and Qi gong: What is the difference? (n.d.). Learn Tai Chi with the Teaptomonk: Courses. Articles, Videos, Books and More. https://www.teapotmonk.com/the-difference-between-taichi-and-qigong.html

Tai Chi Breathing: 9 Guidelines to Improve Practice. (2016, August 1). Tai Chi Basics. https://taichibasics.com/tai-chi-breathing/

Tai Chi Philosophy And Application in Daily Life. (n.d.). Golden Lion Academy. https://www.goldenlion.com.au/tai-chi/history-tai-chi/philosophy/

Taichi — Exercise for Daily Life – Dr. Greg Yuen. (n.d.). Gregyuenmd.com. https://gregyuenmd.com/taichi-exercise-for-daily-life/

The difference between Tai Chi and qi gong. (n.d.). Www.piedmont.org. https://www.piedmont.org/living-better/the-difference-between-tai-chi-and-qi-gong

The Tai Chi Walk - Walking Brush Knee and Press. (2010, June 9). Just Breathe — Tai Chi | Qigong | Yoga. https://zen.thisistruccs.com/2010/06/the-tai-chi-walk-walking-brush-knee-and-press/

The Three Dantians. (2013, July 1). Tai Chi Basics. https://taichibasics.com/three-dantians/

Top 10 Tips For Tai Chi Beginners | realbuzz.com. (n.d.). Realbuzz 5. https://www.realbuzz.com/articles-interests/fitness/article/top-10-tips-for-tai-chi-beginners/

Uhlig, T., Fongen, C., Steen, E., Christie, A., & Ødegård, S. (2010). Exploring Tai Chi in rheumatoid arthritis: a quantitative and qualitative study. BMC musculoskeletal disorders, 11, 43. https://doi.org/10.1186/1471-2474-11-43

Wang, C., Schmid, C. H., Fielding, R. A., Harvey, W. F., Reid, K. F., Price, L. L., Driban, J. B., Kalish, R., Rones, R., & McAlindon, T. (2018). Effect of Tai Chi versus aerobic exercise for fibromyalgia: comparative effectiveness randomized controlled trial. BMJ (Clinical research ed.), 360, k851. https://doi.org/10.1136/bmj.k851

Wang, C., Schmid, C. H., Hibberd, P. L., Kalish, R., Roubenoff, R., Rones, R., & McAlindon, T. (2009). Tai Chi is effective in treating knee osteoarthritis: a randomized controlled trial. Arthritis and rheumatism, 61(11), 1545–1553. https://onlinelibrary.wiley.com/doi/full/10.1002/art.24832

Warm Up and Stretching Exercises | Tai Chi for Health Institute. (2013, December 12). Tai Chi for Health Institute. https://taichiforhealthinstitute.org/warm-up-and-stretching-exercises/

What are the differences between Qigong and Tai Chi? (2017, May 8). Qigong Online by Space to Relax. https://spacetorelax.com/differences-qigong-tai-chi/

What is Tai Chi? | Tai Chi for Health Institute. (2018). Tai Chi for Health Institute. https://taichiforhealthinstitute.org/what-is-tai-chi/

Wu, W., Liu, X., Wang, L., Wang, Z., Hu, J., & Yan, J. (2014). Effects of Tai Chi on exercise capacity and health-related quality of life in patients with chronic obstructive pulmonary disease: a systematic review and meta-analysis. International journal of chronic obstructive pulmonary disease, 9, 1253–1263. https://www.dovepress.com/effects-of-tai-chi-on-exercise-capacity-and-health-related-quality-of--peer-reviewed-fulltext-article-COPD

Yeung, A., Chan, J. S. M., Cheung, J. C., & Zou, L. (2018). Qigong and Tai-Chi for Mood Regulation. FOCUS, 16(1), 40–47. https://focus.psychiatryonline.org/doi/10.1176/appi.focus.20170042

Zheng, S., Kim, C., Lal, S., Meier, P., Sibbritt, D., & Zaslawski, C. (2017). The Effects of Twelve Weeks of Tai Chi Practice on Anxiety in Stressed But Healthy People Compared to Exercise and Wait-List Groups-A Randomized Controlled Trial. Journal of Clinical Psychology, 74(1), 83–92. https://onlinelibrary.wiley.com/doi/abs/10.1002/jclp.22482

"1. What Is the Dantian and Why Is It Important?" Cellular Transformation - Jennifer Millar.

"3 Qigong Breathing Techniques to Practice." Qigong Energy Healing | Powerful Distant Healing - Worldwide.

5 Qigong Exercises and Their Health Benefits | Wight Can Eco. wightcaneco.com/5-Qigong-exercises-and-their-health-benefits/.

"3,000-Year-Old Posture Advice." Toward Harmony Tai Chi & Qigong, https://www.towardharmony.com/on-balance-blog/2018/9/20/3000-year-old-posture-advice.

A Chinese Taoist Diet to Increase Chi Energy - MotleyHealth®. www.motleyhealth.com/diet-and-nutrition/the-taoist-chi-boosting-diet.

"Breathing Techniques - Energy Gates Qigong." Www.energygatesQigong.us,

www.energygatesQigong.us/breathing-techniques.html.

Chong, Dr Jason. "What Is the Dantian? Why Is Lower Dantian Breathing Important?" Dantian Health, 3 Oct. 2014, Dantianhealth.com.au/what-is-the-Dantian/.

Clear, Sigung. "Middle Dan Tien." Clear Tai Chi, 20 Nov. 2009, http://www.clearstaichi.com/dan-tien/middle-dan-tien-1025.html.

"Dantian - an Overview | ScienceDirect Topics." Www.sciencedirect.com,

www.sciencedirect.com/topics/pharmacology-toxicology-and-pharmaceutical-science/Dantian.

"Energy Arts | Learn Tai Chi, Qigong and Meditation." Energy Arts, https://www.energyarts.com/.

"Five Element Framework | TCM World." TCM World, 2019, www.tcmworld.org/what-is-tcm/five-elements/.

Friedlander, Jamie. "What Exactly Is 'Qi'? Plus, 6 Ways to Boost It for Better Health." Healthline, Healthline Media, 25 Feb. 2019, https://www.healthline.com/health/ways-to-balance-qi-for-health.

"Fundamental Eight Stances (Ji Ben Ba Shi)." YMAA, 15 Feb. 2019, ymaa.com/articles/fundamental-eight-stances-ji-ben-ba-shi.

Gong, teaching them the healthy practice of Qi, and adaptation of ACS in their lives. "Dietary Recommendations to Prevent Qi Deficiency - Tai Qi Gong." Tai-Qi-Gong.com, tai-qi-gong.com/dietary-recommendations-prevent-qi-deficiency/.

Gonzalez, Irina. "Imbalanced Chi Energy Could Be the Reason You're so Tired Lately." Oprah Magazine, 8 Apr. 2019, www.oprahmag.com/life/health/a27079502/what-is-chi-energy/.

"Got Jing? Your Overall Health Depends on It!" Activeherb Blog, 16 May 2017, https://www.activeherb.com/blog/what-is-jing-in-tcm.html.

"Home." PetarSmiljana Qigong, petarsmi.com/.

"How to Adopt a Correct Qigong Standing Posture to Promote Free Flow of Qi." Qigong Online by Space to Relax, 4 Oct. 2016, spacetorelax.com/Qigong-standing-posture/.

"How to Increase Inner Calm and Digestive Intelligence by Activating Your Lower Dantian." Calm with Yoga, 11 Feb. 2020, www.calmwithyoga.com/how-to-increase-inner-calm-and-digestive-intelligence-by-activating-your-lower-Dantian/.

"How to Stand during Qigong Practice." Qi Gong for Vitality, 21 Sept. 2018, www.Qigongforvitality.com/stand-Qigong-practice/.

"How to Use Five Elements Wisdom to Guide Your Diet." Holden QiGong, 3 July 2019, www.holdenQigong.com/how-to-use-five-elements-wisdom-to-guide-your-diet/.

"Inner Vitality Qigong - Cleansing Breath." Www.innervitalityQigong.com,

www.innervitalityQigong.com/CleansingBreath.html.

Johnson, Larry. "QiGong for Spiritual Development and Balance." InnerSelf, 20 May 2020,

innerself.com/content/living/health/fitness-and-exercise/5786-Qigong-for-spiritual-development-and-balance.html.

Mantis Project TV. "QiGong Chi Kung Dantian Exercises- Middle Dantian | Mantis Project TV." Mantis Project TV | Tai Chi Chuan-Qigong-Kung Fu-Neigong Tutorials, Mantis Project TV, 3 Jan. 2019, www.mantisproject.tv/eng/qi-gong-Dantian-training-advanced-level/.

McLaughlin, Randy. "Shen Energy: One of Five Types of Energies in Taoist Five Element Theory." RemedyGrove - Holistic Wellness, remedygrove.com/traditional/Shen-Energy-One-of-Five-Types-of-Energies-in-Taoist-Theory.

Nunez, Natalia. "9 Health Benefits of Qigong." Medium, 29 May 2020, medium.com/x-factors-in-life/9-health-benefits-of-Qigong-cc1c76f65098.

Palermo, Elizabeth. "What Is Qigong?" Livescience.com, Live Science, 10 Mar. 2015.

"Qigong | Taking Charge of Your Health & Wellbeing." Taking Charge of Your Health & Wellbeing, 2016, https://www.takingcharge.csh.umn.edu/qigong.

"Qigong Breathing Techniques." Symonds-Yat.co.uk, symonds-yat.co.uk/byu3ntf1/Qigong-breathing-techniques-5281f7.

"Qigong Finger Bending Exercises | Developyourqi.com." Developyourqi.com, developyourqi.com/Qigong-finger-bending-exercises/.

"Qigong Institute - Meditation." Www.Qigonginstitute.org.

"Qigong Meditation for Beginners: What You Need to Know." It's All You Boo, 7 May 2020,

itsallyouboo.com/Qigong-meditation-for-beginners/.

"Qigong Posture Crucial for Rooting & Chi Energy Circulation." Chikung-Unlimited.com, chikung-unlimited.com/posture/.

"Qigong Warm Up." Nature Health, www.naturehealth.com.au/what-is-qi-gong/tiandi-Qigong-basic-routine/Qigong-warm-up/.

"Supreme Science Qigong and Food Based Healing." QiGong, Qigong.com/.

"The Qigong 'Diet.'" Long White Cloud Qigong, 25 May 2019, www.longwhitecloudQigong.com/the-Qigong-diet/.

"The Theory of the Five Elements." Www.springforestQigong.com, www.springforestQigong.com/spring-forest-Qigong/121-theory-of-five-elements.

"This Powerful Daoist Breathing Meditation Deeply Rejuvenates the Body and Mind." Conscious Lifestyle Magazine, 13 Nov. 2015, www.consciouslifestylemag.com/Dantian-daoist-meditation/.

"Three Dantian Meditation." Taoist Sanctuary of San Diego.

Three Intentful Corrections & Principles of Movement – Supercharge Your Life! www.relaxedandalert.com/teacher-training-library/lecture/three-intentful-corrections-principles-of-movement-2.

"Welcome to Taiji Forum - a Universe of Chinese Arts." Taiji Forum, taiji-forum.com/.

"What Are the Health Benefits of Qigong?" Health Essentials from Cleveland Clinic, 23 Sept. 2020,

health.clevelandclinic.org/what-are-the-health-benefits-of-Qigong/.

9 781638 181347